The Fun of Loving Jesus

Embracing the Christianity That Jesus Taught

Roberta Grimes

The Fun of Loving Jesus by: Roberta Grimes

Published by Greater Reality Publications

ISBN: 978-1-7374106-6-9

Printed in the United States of America

Cover picture and design credit: Ratha C. Grimes

This book is dedicated to you.

*May your search for God
reveal to you the glorious truth
of your own divinity.*

TABLE OF CONTENTS

FOREWORD

"He has told you, oh man, what is good; and what does the Lord require of you but to do justice, to love kindness, and to walk humbly with your God?" (Micah 6:8)

— Micah of Moresheth (740BCE-670BCE)

Jesus taught us little that was new! For centuries the Biblical prophets had been bringing the truth to the world's first true monotheists. But in those ancient days it still was assumed that God spoke only in religious terms, so every divine communication soon was muddled by human superstitions. It was the beautiful mission of Jesus to clear away all that was of man, and reveal to us the perfect truth of God. First-century people knew no better than to bury the words of Jesus in yet one more religion, but that has only delayed the moment when Jesus can speak at last and the world will listen.

This book proposes a positive path for disillusioned Christians who might otherwise soon abandon the Jesus of the Gospels. It is an attempt based in prayer and in earnest research to understand after a long and bloody two thousand years what Jesus actually said to us then, and what He hopes that you and I will do now.

If you are delighted with your Christian denomination, this book is not for you. But if you are like so many of us who were raised in the religion, but have increasingly found it to be spiritually wanting, you will be glad to discover that a fresh look at the message of Jesus yields a thrillingly positive Christianity based in God's eternal love that can powerfully transform both your life and the world.

INTRODUCTION

"I did once seriously think of embracing the Christian faith. The gentle figure of Christ, so full of forgiveness that he taught his followers not to retaliate when abused or struck, but to turn the other cheek – I thought it was a beautiful example of the perfect man."

– Mahatma Gandhi,
Indian spiritual activist (1869-1948)

"I believe in God, but not as one thing, not as an old man in the sky. I believe that what people call God is something in all of us. I believe that what Jesus and Mohammed and Buddha and all the rest said was right. It's just that the translations have gone wrong."

– John Lennon, English singer, songwriter,
musician, and peace activist (1940-1980)

"When I do good, I feel good. When I do bad, I feel bad. That's my religion."

– Abraham Lincoln,
16th president of the United States (1809-1865)

"I love you when you bow in your mosque, kneel in your temple, pray in your church. For you and I are sons of one religion, and it is the spirit."

– Kahlil Gibran,
Lebanese writer, poet, and artist (1883-1931)

"Since many of you do not belong to the Catholic Church and others are non-believers, from the bottom of my heart I give this silent blessing to each and every one of you, respecting the conscience of each one of you but knowing that each one of you is a child of God."

– Pope Francis, 266th Pontiff of the Catholic Church

"Of all the systems of morality, ancient or modern which have come under my observation, none appears to me so pure as that of Jesus.... I am a real Christian, that is to say, a disciple of the doctrines of Jesus."

– Thomas Jefferson,
3rd president of the United States (1743-1826)

1

*F*or thousands of years humankind has seen religions as both essential and useful. For most of human history we have lived in a complex reality that we could not begin to understand, and religions have given us a moral direction, a basis for community grounding, and rituals that let us feel more in control. The fact that religions still persist despite all their cost in time and treasure indicates that the fears that once made them necessary still persist over most of the world; but thanks to people we used to think were dead, we have the power now to address those fears. And for reasons this book will detail for you, our old religions have become such a drag on human spiritual progress that this is likely to be the final century in which we will practice any religions at all.

We will be talking here about Christianity, but every religion has the same limitations. And the death of traditional Christian dogmas will free powerful teachings that can transform the world, just as will the deaths of the other world religions as they are currently being practiced free the transformative teachings of Lao-tzu, Krishna, the Buddha, and so many other spiritual teachers whose wisdom still is buried in superstitions and is for the most part ignored.

Please understand that I am not trying to bring about the end of religions! I seek only to explain to you why there is nothing that we can do to prevent the extinction of all the great religions as we now practice them, and why their demise will be a good thing. As a child eventually gets past crawling and begins to stand up on its own, so humankind is maturing spiritually. What will follow the death of religions will be a much closer walk with the genuine God, and a birth of universal love and human unity over all the earth.

Understanding What is Wrong with Religions

As the Christian Bible tells us, **"To everything there is a season, and a time for every purpose under heaven"** (Eccl 3:1). For millennia religions have been a useful frame on which to hang our primitive interpretations of non-material reality while we allayed our fears of the unknown. But religions are just human inventions. No matter what we might tell ourselves, no religion ever came from God! And of late our religions have become so destructive of the spiritual unity of humankind that if they were not dying on their own, we would need to begin to find ways to fight free of them. Let's look at just five of the many problems that all religions share:

1) **Religions are divisive.** Each espouses a different set of beliefs, and those beliefs have been interpreted and then reinterpreted over the ages as all the great religions have splintered into sects that often are at odds with one another. There are now more than forty-two thousand versions of Christianity alone! And given what we have come to understand about how reality works, we know now that any force that so destructively divides humankind is counterproductive and morally wrong.

2) **Religions are stuck in the past.** Each of our great religions was founded around a central figure who brought to us what we are now able to confirm by means of recent evidence were versions of eternal truths. But those truths were soon distorted into superstitions and encased in cultural accretions from the time and place of each religion's founding, and all that superstitious and cultural baggage remains encrusted on our religions to this day. Each set of precious spiritual teachings has become like an ancient fly in amber: still preserved, but now inaccessible because the religion itself is in the way.

3) **Religions are based in superstitious fears.** I know of no
religion that does not use fear as its core human motivator.
Generally they use the fear of God, fear of hell, or just fear of
negative personal outcomes to keep the pews warm and the
money flowing. And as you will see, the fact that religions
generate and run on fear contributes substantially to the
ongoing debasement of humankind. It makes our spiritual
growth impossible, and it actually puts our planet at risk.

4) **Religions require that we accept dogmas.** And since those
dogmas are centuries or even millennia old, it is impossible for
any religion to evolve. At best, a few have undergone
"reformations" and spawned a more relaxed sect or two, but
still nearly all the core dogmas remain. There is no religion of
which I am aware that encourages its followers to challenge, to
seek, and to explore! And this is sadly true of Christianity as
well, even though Jesus urged us to do all three: He said, "**So
I say to you, ask, and it will be given to you; seek, and you
will find; knock, and it will be opened to you. For everyone
who asks, receives; and he who seeks, finds; and to him who
knocks, it will be opened**" (LK 11:9-10). We consider human
progress to be desirable in every other aspect of our complex
cultures. But when it comes to our spiritual lives, we take being
stuck at an ancient developmental level to be just fine.

5) **Every Christian dogma can now be demonstrated to be
wrong.** It is not surprising to learn that they all are wrong,
since they were established so long ago! But information
gleaned over the past two centuries from people that we used
to think were dead has at last revealed to us the truth about
God, and that is a game-changer for all religions. In Appendix
V I will show you the human errors at the core of sixteen
Christian dogmas, and the same sort of analysis can be made

of the dogmas espoused by every other religion. We generally find that the revered leader around whom each religion was built had it right, but the followers who built that religion were clueless, wrong, and sometimes venal.

Every modern religion is little more than a set of ancient superstitions. They have served humanity for thousands of years when no source of truth was available to us; and if we still had no further options, they could probably continue to serve us today. But the plain fact is that we have now for some wonderfully positive reasons managed to outgrow any need for religions! Our religions still stumble on as the zombies that they are, but they grow weaker by the day. And once we can move past them, the shining new day of worldwide love and harmony that was long ago prophesied by Jesus and by other of the greatest prophets can at long last begin to dawn.

Knowing that all of this is going to kill the religion that I still love has given me an urgent wish to build on the ashes of those forty-two thousand wrong denominations the one pure Christian movement that Jesus tells us He actually came to earth to begin. His divine mission is clear in the Gospels, but few Christians seem to read the Gospels, and most of those who do read them use other parts of the Bible to modify the Lord's Gospel words. It is time now to do what you will see that Jesus is directing us to do, and throw away both the entire Old Testament and the balance of the New Testament. Once the Gospels are free of the rest of the Bible, those four books that carry the teachings of Jesus provide a blueprint for a genuine Christianity that is no longer bound by fear-based dogmas, but instead is the sharing of the perfect truths of the genuine God with all the world. As you will see, modern Christians have much to celebrate!

CHAPTER ONE
THE SORRY STATE OF
CHRISTIANITY TODAY

"I believe in mysticism, with an interior goal, and you are your own temple and your own priest. I don't believe anymore in religions, because you see today there are religious wars, prejudice, false morals, and the woman is despised. Religion is too old now; it's from another century, it's not for today."

– Alejandro Jodorowsky, Chilean-French director, author, musician, and spiritual guru

"Religious tolerance is something we should all practice; however, there have been more persecution and atrocities committed in the name of religion and religious freedom than anything else."

– Walter Koenig, American actor, writer, teacher and director

"There are things about organized religion which I resent. Christ is revered as the Prince of Peace, but more blood has been shed in His name than any other figure in history. You show me one step forward in the name of religion, and I'll show you a hundred retrogressions."

– Frank Sinatra, American singer, actor, and producer (1915-1998)

"When the missionaries came to Africa they had the Bible and we had the land. They said 'Let us pray.' We closed our eyes. When we opened them we had the Bible and they had the land."

– Desmond Tutu, South African social rights activist and Anglican bishop (1931-2021)

"I feel much freer now that I am certain the pope is the Antichrist."

– Martin Luther, German theologian, composer, priest, and monk (1483-1546)

"Rogueries, absurdities and untruths were perpetrated upon the teachings of Jesus by a large band of dupes and importers led by Paul, the first great corrupter of the teaching of Jesus."

– Thomas Jefferson, 3rd president of the United States (1743-1826)

F or most of my life I have been a devout traditional
      Christian. I was reading the Bible daily by my early teens,
      from cover to cover and over and over, and I majored in
early Christian history in college. I assumed I would become a
minister, but then I fell in love with and married a Catholic so I was
a zealous Catholic for twenty-five years. I still love Christianity
with everything in me, the hymns and the pageantry, and perhaps
above all the sweet certainty of always knowing as that wafer
melted on my tongue that I had sealed myself to God for another
week.

*I tell you this so you will understand how hard this journey
has been for me.* Had I been less curious, I'm sure I would be an
ardent Catholic to this day, still wincing a bit at the thought of a
Father Who could demand the blood-sacrifice of His own Son,
while remaining certain that Christianity was right. But when I was
a child, I also had two deeply spiritual experiences of light that led
me to begin a fifty-year search for the afterlife. I had to figure out
how and why those experiences had happened! What on earth
(and in heaven) was going on?

My Discovery That Jesus is Real

*I spent decades in studying nearly two hundred years of
abundant and consistent afterlife evidence.* This was an advantage
that no one in history before the early twentieth century could have
had, this ready access to detailed communications from people that
we used to think were dead. And the picture the dead painted was
so consistent and complete that by my fifties I was absolutely
certain that God is real, human minds are eternal, and learning to
love is the purpose of our lives. Let me tell you, having faith is
good, but being certain is a great deal better!

Of course, while I was trying to understand reality, I also was looking for happy confirmation that the things I had believed as a Christian were true. And as I became more certain that God is real and human life is eternal, I also was becoming ever more convinced that nothing I had believed as a Christian could have any basis in truth at all. I was in my fifties when I gave up my search for validation of the religion that I loved, and all I recall now is my fear in that moment. I hadn't set out to discover that Christianity is bogus. Could you even go to hell for learning something like that? I stopped reading my Bible and the afterlife communications literature on the same sad day, and I spent the better part of the next two years just living my life and going to church and trying to pretend that none of it had happened.

My only solace lay in my knowledge that in truth there was **something** *behind that curtain.* And since I knew the Gospels almost by heart, I was comforted to know that much of what Jesus had said had been confirmed by the recently dead. But at this point, Jesus was all I had left! I couldn't bear to open my Bible again and find all the places where He had said things that I was going to be able to prove now were wrong. It took me most of those traumatic two years to work up the courage to dust off my Bible and once again read the Gospel words of Jesus.

I recall that rainy day as if it was yesterday. With apologies to my husband and children, it was the most wonderful day of my life. I was cringing during most of my reading, awaiting that first blow of discovering that the Lord had made this or that big mistake; but instead of finding discrepancies with the afterlife evidence, I found page after page of confirmations.

I think it was the story of the woman at the well that sealed the deal for me. I had found so many places where the Gospel text agreed with what the dead had been telling us, and I hadn't been bothered by anachronistic bits because I knew the Council of Nicaea had edited all four Gospels in the year 325 CE. (This gives you some idea of the lack of reverence in which the Church Fathers held the words of Jesus. Among other things, they removed what references they could find to reincarnation, and they inserted references to end-times prophesies and church-building that stick out as inconsistent with the rest of the Lord's Gospel words.)

What I feared to find was evidence that Jesus had taught what I now knew to be wrong, that He had talked about His dying for our sins or God's judgment or the notion that God condemns us to hell forever, or perhaps His saying somewhere that only Christians go to heaven. But there was none of that. I recall my delight as I realized that I was better understanding His Gospel words in light of the testimony of the not-really-dead. And then I came to this amazing moment!

Jesus was speaking to the Samaritan woman at the well who was drawing up water for Him to drink. "And Jesus answered and said to her, **'If you knew the gift of God, and who it is who says to you, "Give Me a drink," you would have asked Him, and He would have given you living water'"** (JN 4:10).

Living water! One thing people tell us from the afterlife levels is that the water there is *alive*. It looks like water, but it feels dry as silk, and it gives off music and an amazing rejuvenating energy. And Jesus, sitting by that well, knew all about the living water. After an afternoon of finding so many validations, I don't know why this was the one that did it for me, but I knew then that a genuine Jesus had walked the earth two thousand years ago knowing things that He could not have known if He had not been precisely who He said He was. He had told us things about God, reality, death, the afterlife, and the meaning and purpose of human life that we could not have validated until at least the early twentieth century. *Jesus is real!* On that day, my absolute devotion to the Lord was sealed.

Accepting the Fact That Christian Dogmas Are Nonsense

One problem with learning the wonderful truth that Jesus agrees with what the dead now tell us is that we also must face the fact that the dead insist to us the Christian dogmas are wrong. People think of Christian beliefs as a package, but in fact they can be divided into two baskets: there are the things that Jesus taught in the Gospels, and then there are all the other notions that came from first-century Jewish beliefs, from the New Testament letters of Paul, from the eight councils held during the first millennium, and from another millennium of further human accretions. It is all those non-Gospel teachings that are behind nearly everything that modern Christians believe, while the teachings of Jesus are generally seen by Christians to be merely aspirational. And it was only as I came to see that Jesus and His teachings are genuine that I was able to see this Christian emphasis on the non-Gospel dogmas as the travesty that it is. The Gospels show us Jesus doing His perfect and world-transforming work; and then He dies, and we can watch fallible human beings building the disastrously flawed Christianity that survives to this day.

An exposition of all the many ways in which modern Christianity is demonstrably wrong would be too distracting to give to you here, so instead Appendix V lists sixteen core bogus Christian beliefs and shares with you what is now understood by researchers with open minds to be the truth of them. Most people who read this book won't need to see such refutations in order to be comfortable with contemplating fresh ideas. But if you ever feel uneasy about anything that you read here, you might find that pausing and reading Appendices III, IV, and V will give you a helpful grounding.

It Is Time to Unwrap the Lord's Gift

Please don't get me wrong. I am grateful to Paul and to the Christian Fathers! Jesus insisted that we not package His teachings in first-century Judaism or in other old beliefs when he said, **"But no one puts a patch of unshrunk cloth on an old garment; for the patch pulls away from the garment, and a worse tear results. Nor do people put new wine into old wineskins; otherwise the wineskins burst, and the wine pours out and the wineskins are ruined"** (MT 9:16-17). But the earliest Christians faced such tremendous persecution that if Paul and the others had not packaged the teachings of Jesus in a new religion, those teachings probably would have been altogether lost.

So Christianity has wonderfully preserved for us the perfect Gospel teachings of Jesus. And just as is true of any protective covering, there was bound to come a better day when we could unwrap our wonderful gift! Tragically, though, the Council of Nicaea proclaimed as they assembled the first Christian Bible that their back-room negotiations were inspired by God, so now many modern Christians believe that in the year 325 we received the last word that God ever will give to us. Does this mean that you and I must accept the inconsistent and sometimes barbaric book of disparate writings that we call The Good Book as God's Inspired Word for all time?

Of course not. For human beings to attempt to deny God the right to give us new revelation negates what the dead now tell us is true: God is real, God is eternal, God is infinitely powerful, and God is perfect love. As human civilization has progressed over the past two millennia, our understanding in scientific and cultural areas likewise has progressed by light-years! So why does it not make sense that God might now want to bring to modern people a greater and deeper spiritual understanding than what the first-century primitives who heard Jesus speak could have comprehended? Indeed, Jesus Himself anticipated that later generations were going to need more information. He said, **"Ask, and it will be given to you; seek, and you will find; knock, and it will be opened to you. For everyone who asks receives, and he who seeks finds, and to him who knocks it will be opened"** (MT 7:7-8). The plain fact is that with these words the Lord invited you and me to seek Him today beyond the boundaries of the Christian Bible.

Traditional Christianity is in Rapid Decline

While European Christians were falling away from the faith by the end of the Second World War, we have long believed that the United States remained a staunchly Christian nation. We now realize, however, that behind their façade of resolute Christian orthodoxy, our churches have been hollowing out. It is estimated that since the nineteen-sixties, this nation's six largest Protestant denominations have lost more than half their membership. Yes, some of these folks have wearied of hellfire and moved on to Unity churches and other more upbeat modes of worship, or perhaps to prosperity mega-churches; but many people born into Christianity simply have given up on religion. Recent surveys by respected

Christian pollster George Barna suggest that at this point, only four percent of America's teenagers are traditional Christians by profession and worldview. Among their grandparents, only about a third now see themselves as traditional Christians, and forty-three percent of all Americans admit that they never attend any church at all. So the recent falling-away from traditional Christian beliefs in the world's most devoutly Christian nation has been dramatic.

Where Jesus is concerned, the news is better. An earlier Barna survey found that more than nine out of ten American adults believed that Jesus was a real person, and that percentage hasn't gone down much, even among the very young. Surprisingly, nearly sixty percent of Americans still say that Jesus was God on earth. And surveys taken in the year of this book's first publication find that Jesus is still the first or second most popular individual worldwide.

Suggesting Revulsion as One Reason for Traditional Christianity's Decline

As I have begun to write about the ways in which our dead communicators affirm the Gospel truths, while they also tell us Christian dogmas are nonsense, I have been hearing from more and more of those who have abandoned traditional Christianity. I have asked many of them why they made the leap, and their reasons generally have boiled down to three. I wish now that I had been keeping track of how many people offered each explanation, but here are the three answers usually given, in what I think is their descending order:

- *They have begun to find Christian teachings hard to believe.* Many people have said some variant of this, and of course my own quibble has been to wonder how an all-powerful and perfectly loving God could demand the blood-sacrifice of His own child. Christianity's dogmas were set in stone more than sixteen hundred years ago, and to more and more sophisticated moderns they look like the barbaric nonsense that in fact they are.

- **They found too many of the Christians in their old churches to be off-putting.** The fact that Christian dogmas are based in fear creates a disconnect for practicing Christians, since some might aspire to follow the teachings of Jesus, but the fear that keeps them in their pews tends to make them feel more self-righteous and judgmental and less loving. In later chapters we will be exploring how the physics of spirituality works, and why a fear-based religion too often produces people you would rather not be around. But for now, suffice it to say that there are good reasons why so few modern Christians bear much resemblance to Jesus Christ.

- **Christianity doesn't follow the teachings of Jesus.** I have heard this from a few thoughtful people who had met the genuine Jesus in the Gospels and had then come to reject Christianity because it ignores the truths that Jesus taught. As someone who also hungers for a much closer spiritual walk with Jesus, I understand how they feel! The more you read the Gospels, the more impatient you become with all the dogmas and the pageantry and fluff of Christianity. You realize that it has nothing to do with Him.

The fact that the Christianity that was largely assembled in and soon after the year 325 included a lot of mistaken beliefs is understandable. The Council of Nicaea was a creature of its time, and the clerics who were there knew nothing about what nearly seventeen hundred years of further human development has revealed since those ancient worthies laid down their pens. The error lies not with the Christian Fathers, but it lies instead in the fact that despite the Lord's insistence that we keep searching for the truth, and His promise that God would continue to reveal it to us, Christianity soon made it a core belief that God would never again tell us anything.

Liberating Jesus

To get to the place where I am now, the knowledge and the certainty, all I had to do was ask. For the past seventeen hundred years, Jesus has been anxious to fix Christianity, but it is in the nature of our lives on earth that Spirit will not break in and dictate anything. Then I asked, and in April of 2009 I gave my life to God. In 2015 I was used by Jesus to write *Liberating Jesus*, and I can recommend that book without reservation because I was there when it was written so I can assure you that I did not write it. I vividly recall the Voice in my mind that said, **"This is My new Revelation."** My heart ached for Him then, because His "new revelation" is precisely the same as His old revelation. I heard His voice clearly in my mind when He said, **"You say you are following Me? Then *listen* to Me!"**

The fact that the Christian dogmas are bogus has been catching up with traditional Christianity. It had to happen! Those who are not now in bodies and have achieved the highest levels of reality have been working through thousands of people on earth for at least the past century to raise the human consciousness of this planet. All over the world, religious people are being reached by their own guides and touched with the truth, so religions in general are under siege, and they are going in one of two directions. Either they are doubling down on fear in order to keep their hold on people, or they are seeing their pews empty and their influence wane. The most strictly fundamentalist Christian sects are deeply based in Old Testament fear, so they seem to be holding up somewhat better; but it has been estimated that the six largest Protestant denominations lost a quarter of their membership between 1965 and 1990. Surveys show that more and more people each year are professing themselves to be "spiritual but not religious."

The field of our hearts is being cleared for fresh seeding.

Almost since the day that *Liberating Jesus* was first published, people who have read it have been saying to me some variant of, "Okay, we get that Christianity is going down, but what will replace it? What are people who want to follow Jesus going to do?" I always told them I had no idea. It is only now that it dawns on me that what will follow the death of every variant of traditional Christianity will be a single *Jesus-based* Christianity. If anyone deserves the honored title of "Christian," it is those who seek to follow Jesus Christ alone! And for you and me, our responsibility and our joy will be to give to our beloved Master finally, after two thousand years, the movement that He came to earth to begin.

He said, **"The kingdom of heaven is like leaven, which a woman took and hid in three pecks of flour until it was all leavened"** (MT 13:33). Those of us who follow only Jesus are being called now to be the leaven in the loaf, and to spread the Lord's truth to every Christian until all that will survive of Christianity will be what is of God and not of man.

Daring To Question That Old-Time Religion

CHAPTER TWO
BEGINNING TO COMPREHEND OUR
GREATER REALITY

"If at first the idea is not absurd, then there is no hope for it."
— Albert Einstein, German-born
winner of the 1921 Nobel Prize in Physics (1879-1955)

"Science is not only compatible with spirituality; it is a profound source of spirituality... The notion that science and spirituality are somehow mutually exclusive does a disservice to both."
— Carl Sagan, American astronomer,
cosmologist, and astrophysicist (1934-1996)

"The world is full of people who have never, since childhood, met an open doorway with an open mind."
— E. B. White, American writer (1899-1985)

"We have no right to assume that any physical laws exist, or if they have existed up to now, that they will continue to exist in a similar manner in the future."
— Max Planck, German
winner of the 1918 Nobel Prize in Physics (1858-1947)

"Bad religion is arrogant, self-righteous, dogmatic and intolerant. And so is bad science. But unlike religious fundamentalists, scientific fundamentalists do not realize that their opinions are based on faith. They think they know the truth."
— Rupert Sheldrake,
British author and parapsychologist

"He who knows nothing is closer to the truth than he whose mind is filled with falsehoods and errors."
— Thomas Jefferson
3rd President of the United States (1743-1826)

*I*t isn't only Christianity that cleaves to dogmas which keep it stuck in the past, but mainstream science has the same problem. The best and most abundant communications that we ever have received from the dead came in the late nineteenth century and in the first part of the twentieth century, precisely when scientists were reeling from the sudden advent of quantum mechanics. Soon researchers were transcribing amazing afterlife communications received through deep-trance and other physical mediums in southern England and in the eastern United States, producing books and papers and expecting mainstream scientists to join them in their investigations. But while scientists were trying to puzzle out how quantum mechanics might fit with classical physics, the last thing they were prepared to do was consider the possibility that we were hearing from dead people!

So about a hundred years ago, the scientific gatekeepers – the university departments and the peer-reviewed journals – established materialism as what they called "the fundamental scientific dogma." And yes, back then you could find those words in print. Even more than a century later, no scientist who hopes for a respectable mainstream career can be seen to be studying anything that might suggest that reality is not material; and this is true, even though such venerable scientists as Albert Einstein have tried to help them realize that in fact there is no such thing as solid matter. Einstein said, "Concerning matter, we have been all wrong. What we have called matter is energy, whose vibration has been so lowered as to be perceptible to the senses. There is no matter." And he said, "It followed from the special theory of relativity that mass and energy are both but different manifestations of the same thing — a somewhat unfamiliar conception for the average mind."

All of this is what afterlife researchers have been learning from the dead as well! But rather than open their minds at all, mainstream scientists have ignored Dr. Einstein's insights, just as they have ignored Max Planck's. Dr. Planck was the father of quantum mechanics, for which he won the 1918 Nobel Prize in Physics; and his work led him to reach Einstein's conclusions about matter's insubstantiality. **In 1944 he said, "As a man who has devoted his whole life to the most clear headed science, to the study of matter, I can tell you as a result of my research about atoms this much: There is no matter as such. All matter originates and exists only by virtue of a force which brings the particle of an atom to vibration and holds this most minute solar system of the atom together. We must assume behind this force the existence of a conscious and intelligent mind. This mind is the matrix of all matter."**

Mainstream Scientific Inquiry Has Become a Belief-System

Our greatest scientists knew a century ago that there is no such thing as solid matter, but to this day no mainstream scientist can expand on these discoveries because that old materialist dogma remains in place as the scientific gatekeepers' bulwark against the entirely imaginary horrors of theism. Their basing of physics in the study of matter ensures that no scientist will discover God. Sadly, these people think they are fighting the bogus beliefs of human-made religions; instead, though, for the past century they have been fighting the objective truth.

Of course, every discipline that enforces a dogma is a belief-system. It preserves whatever is the current state of knowledge in that particular field as an inviolate belief, allowing no consideration of later insights that might contradict that sacred dogma. We expect religions to be based in ancient ideas, so the fact that Christians refuse to consider any more recent developments seems to many to be not a vice, but a virtue.

Scientific inquiry, however, is another matter. Until scientists are free to study all of reality objectively, mainstream science will be stuck in old ideas; and so in fact it has been stuck, and for more than a century. In all that time we have had considerable medical and technological advances, but the core scientific discipline of physics has produced only ever more untestable theories. As the great Nikola Tesla said, **"The day science begins to study non-physical phenomena, it will make more progress in one decade than in all the previous centuries of its existence."** But physicists have ignored him, too.

The harm that has been done to scientific inquiry by the introduction more than a century ago of that ill-considered "fundamental scientific dogma of materialism" is a topic beyond the scope of this book, but expect it to become a controversial issue within the next few decades as methods for clearer and more reliable electronic communication with those that we used to think were dead begin to go mainstream.

Scientific Revelations from the Not-Really-Dead

The dead know a great deal more than we do. From their elevated eternal perspective, those of the dead who are better developed spiritually can not only tell us why we are here, but they also seem to be able to "game out" and predict from present trends what are the most likely future events. A lot of solid information about the afterlife and the greater reality is now available in print, and if you are not yet certain that we survive our deaths, please educate yourself! Appendices I and II give you a place to begin.

I don't know how important knowledge of the greater reality that is most of reality is going to be to your more rapid spiritual growth, but I strongly suspect that it helps. Better understanding the truth frees us from fears and superstitions, and knowing how much your degree of spiritual development will matter after you die is going to inspire you to want to grow spiritually. But if your time is tight, then simply assume for now that open-minded researchers have it right, and you can fill in the gaps in your knowledge later.

The higher-level dead who communicate with us are telling us a great deal more than just the fact that human minds are eternal. What afterlife researchers have begun to glimpse is a greater reality that is many times the size of this whole physical universe, complex and astounding and based in love! And insofar as we are able to determine, all of it is created and governed by an infinitely powerful variant of what we experience as human consciousness. Here are a few important facts that the dead consistently share:

- *The only thing that is objectively real is an infinitely powerful and infinitely creative consciousness-based and energy-like potentiality without size or form, alive in the sense that your mind is alive, highly emotional and therefore probably self-aware.* God, in other words. Everything else that we think is real is an artifact of that energy-like potentiality. Credit for the scientific discovery of the base consciousness energy that is the genuine God goes to pioneering quantum physicist Max Planck. In 1931 Dr. Planck said, "I regard consciousness as fundamental. I regard matter as derivative from consciousness. We cannot get behind consciousness. Everything that we talk about, everything that we regard as existing, postulates consciousness." But the problem for Christians is that the genuine God bears no resemblance to the Christian God, and in fact there is no evidence for a human-like God that feels anger or jealousy or the need to judge us. Instead, the base consciousness that is all that exists seems to be what Jesus calls Spirit.

- *All human minds are part of the base creative energy that is all that exists.* Not as separate dots, mind you, but rather as inextricable parts of one whole. So the sense we have that our minds are generated by our brains is just an illusion that may be based on nothing more than the fact that our organs for sight and hearing are on our heads.

- *There is almost no religion practiced in the afterlife levels.* Just as there are no atheists in heaven, so also there are no religionists, beyond the fact that people might sing hymns for nostalgia's sake. People don't need faith when they live in certainty.

- *Jesus is much more important in the afterlife levels than He is here.* They call him the Master, and He is a powerful spiritual center, loved and revered more than you can imagine. The Buddha also is sometimes reported, but he is not seen as comparable to Jesus. In fact, there is some evidence that the Master may be the most advanced being in every dimension and in every universe. While all of us are part of the Mind of God, consciousness exists in a range of vibrations from fear at the bottom to love at the top. And we are told that Master Jesus is of the highest aspect of the Godhead, which is why I now capitalize His pronouns.

A Few Words About God

It is ironic that advocates of scientific inquiry and advocates of religious worship have battled one another for centuries about which view of reality will prevail, when in fact neither of them has it right. The cranky human-like Christian God does not exist. Instead, the only thing that exists is an infinitely loving Power that continuously gives rise to everything else, which means that scientists who still want to think that reality is random are off-track, too.

Dr. Planck called the base consciousness Mind. It includes all of our minds, and in its most spiritually perfected form it is the Godhead Collective which continuously manifests this universe. Our current understanding is that above all realities there also is an ultimate High God, although our knowledge at that level is limited. You might think of Mind as the genuine, modern, enlightened, improved, and very much more wonderful version of what God always has been; although for thousands of years people could not have begun to understand the nature of the genuine God. So if you are an atheist, please be assured that no human-like version of God exists. If you are religious, you can come home with joy to the certainty that God is all-powerful love, and you in particular are God's best-beloved child.

The Afterlife Evidence Affirms the Teachings of Jesus

Without the testimony of the dead, we would not be able to confirm that the Gospel words of Jesus are true. Two thousand years ago, Jesus told us things about God, reality, death, the afterlife, and the meaning and purpose of our lives that we could not have validated by any means until we first had put together a thorough account of what the dead are telling us, which happened late in the twentieth century.

In Appendix IV I outline some of the astonishing correspondences between what Jesus said two thousand years ago and what the dead are telling us now. Given the difficult road that the teachings of Jesus have had to travel in order to be with us at all, even garbled, the fact that they turn out to be so consistent with an independent, verifiable source of information may eventually be seen to amount to nothing less than a new revelation from God.

CHAPTER THREE
OUR COMPELLING NEED FOR
SPIRITUAL GROWTH

"You cannot teach a man anything; you can only help him find it within himself."

– Galileo Galilei, Italian polymath (1564-1642)

"Watch your thoughts, for they become words. Watch your words, for they become actions. Watch your actions, for they become habits. Watch your habits, for they become character. Watch your character, for it becomes your destiny."

– Mahatma Gandhi,
Indian spiritual activist (1869-1948)

"A commonsense interpretation of the facts suggests that a superintellect has monkeyed with physics, as well as with chemistry and biology, and that there are no blind forces worth speaking about in nature. The numbers one calculates from the facts seem to me so overwhelming as to put this conclusion almost beyond question."

– Fred Hoyle,
English mathematician and astronomer (1915-2001)

"We do not have to visit a madhouse to find disordered minds; our planet is the mental institution of the universe."

– Johann Wolfgang von Goethe,
German writer and statesman (1749-1832)

"Do not grow old, no matter how long you live. Never cease to stand like curious children before the great mystery into which we were born."

– Albert Einstein, German-born
winner of the 1921 Nobel Prize in Physics (1879-1955)

"I believe in both a creative and personal God, a divinely ordered universe, that man has an innate moral sense, and that Jesus was a great moral teacher, perhaps the greatest the world has witnessed."

– Thomas Jefferson,
3rd president of the United States (1743-1826)

*T*wo thousand years ago Jesus gave us the answer to what has been humankind's oldest question. Why do we live lives on earth? Jesus told us we are here to learn to love perfectly and learn to forgive completely. And now, thanks to recent communications from people that we used to think were dead, we can confirm that the answer Jesus gave us is right.

Dead communicators uniformly say that we come into lives on earth in order to experience low-vibration consciousness so we can grow spiritually away from fear and toward more perfect love. Afterlife researchers are coming to conclude that this material universe is something like a school, or perhaps it is a spiritual gym where we can experience and struggle against a negativity that does not exist in the afterlife. Of course, this concept does raise one big question. Since our minds are part of God, and God is perfect, why aren't you and I already perfect? A preliminary answer seems to be that while we are of the same consciousness as God, we must work to elevate our personal energies farther away from fear and closer to love in order to more perfectly unite with God and unite with one another.

The Miracle of the Lord's Gospel Revelations

The fact that we are here to raise our personal vibrations away from fear and toward love is stated repeatedly by Jesus in the Gospels. That He risked execution for speaking so plainly shows how important these truths are to Him. And that the answers He gave are so clear is even more amazing when you think about the long odds that exist against our having today even an approximation of what He said!

Let's look at some of the obstacles the Gospel truths have had to surmount in order to be available to us today:

- *For Jesus to have spoken directly against the prevailing religion would have meant a prompt death sentence.* He managed to stay alive for more than three years while He was teaching subversion by speaking in parables, giving pieces of truths over days of time and expecting His listeners to put them together, and frequently quoting those Jewish scriptural passages that were consistent with the truth and then adding His own subversive twist. What is notable for us is that apparently Jesus quoted very little of the Old Testament, and when He quoted it He often edited what He said. Appendix IV will give you some examples of the artful ways in which Jesus taught the truth when He could not have spoken about it plainly.

- *Jesus spoke Aramaic. His words were translated into Greek, and from Greek into modern languages.* What is astonishing about this fact is that the words that Jesus is quoted as saying in a modern English translation of the Bible about love, forgiveness, the nature of God, and the meaning and purpose of human life are so consistent with what the dead are now telling us! Again, check out Appendix IV.

- *The Gospels were extensively edited.* The Council of Nicaea, in particular, removed what references to reincarnation it could find, and it added scary words about end-times and church-building that the historical Jesus never uttered. Appendix IV includes some examples.

The literal miracle here is the fact that a modern English translation of the Gospels from Aramaic to Greek and from Greek into English is much more similar to what we are learning from those that we used to think were dead than is a Gospel translation made from Aramaic directly into English. I have been puzzling over this amazing fact for years! And my first conclusion remains the most likely explanation: those two-step modern translations must have been supervised by advanced beings. They are indeed God's new revelation.

Our Pressing Need for Spiritual Growth

Jesus talks often in the Gospels about spiritual growth, and a close reading of his Gospel words is important. We cannot be followers of Jesus unless we internalize and live by what He said. He tells us to put the success of His effort to bring the Kingdom of God on earth foremost in our prayers when He teaches us to begin each prayer to God in this way: **"Our Father who is in heaven, Hallowed (or holy, or revered) be Your name. Your kingdom come. Your will be done, On earth as it is in heaven"** (MT 6:9-10). Then He patiently calls us throughout the Gospels to learn to love ever more perfectly, telling us to **"love your enemies and pray for those who persecute you, so that you may be sons of your Father who is in heaven… you are to be perfect, as your heavenly Father is perfect"** (MT 5:43-48).

He tells us that the Kingdom of God will begin with us, but will grow amazingly. **"How shall we picture the kingdom of God, or by what parable shall we present it? It is like a mustard seed, which, when sown upon the soil, though it is smaller than all the seeds that are upon the soil, yet when it is sown, it grows up and becomes larger than all the garden plants and forms large branches"** (MK 4:30-32).

First-century Jews could not have known why learning to love perfectly was so important, but we know now that what we experience in a more limited way as human consciousness is the base creative force that continuously manifests reality.

Afterlife researchers, open-minded physicists, and the not-really-dead agree that the core spiritual energy that we experience as consciousness is the source of everything that we think of as real. Consciousness is something like a form of energy, and as is true of all energy, it vibrates. Its vibratory range is from the slowest, which is fear, hatred, and all the other ishy emotions, to the highest vibration, which is perfect love. Do you see how this all fits together? Jesus told us two thousand years ago that we are here to learn to love more perfectly, and – sure enough! – He was perfectly right.

So anything that fosters love over fear is going to be productive for us, but anything that creates or intensifies fear is going to retard our spiritual growth. That fact is a problem for all religions, and particularly so for the primary forms of Christianity that are still being practiced today.

Chapters Seven through Nine will show you more of what Jesus means by love, forgiveness, and the kingdom of God, but suffice it to say for now that the more perfectly we can love, the higher will become our personal spiritual vibratory rate. *And when even a small fraction of living people have sufficiently raised their personal vibrations away from fear and toward more perfect love, we will have brought the kingdom of God on earth.*

CHAPTER FOUR
SUPERSTITIOUS FEARS ARE
SPIRITUALLY HARMFUL

"A human being is a part of the whole called by us universe, a part limited in time and space. He experiences himself, his thoughts and feeling as something separated from the rest, a kind of optical delusion of his consciousness. This delusion is a kind of prison for us, restricting us to our personal desires and to affection for a few persons nearest to us. Our task must be to free ourselves from this prison by widening our circle of compassion to embrace all living creatures and the whole of nature in its beauty."

– Albert Einstein, German-born
winner of the 1921 Nobel Prize in Physics (1879-1955)

"The course does not aim at teaching the meaning of love, for that is beyond what can be taught. It does aim, however, at removing the blocks to the awareness of love's presence, which is your natural inheritance. The opposite of love is fear, but what is all-encompassing can have no opposite."

– A Course in Miracles, Introduction

"There are trivial truths and there are great truths. The opposite of a trivial truth is plainly false. The opposite of a great truth is also true."

– Niels Bohr, Danish
winner of the 1922 Nobel prize in Physics (1885-1962)

"Never doubt that a small group of thoughtful, committed citizens can change the world; indeed, it's the only thing that ever has."

– Margaret Mead,
American cultural anthropologist (1901-1978)

"As human beings, our greatness lies not so much in being able to remake the world – that is the myth of the atomic age – as in being able to remake ourselves."

– Mahatma Gandhi, Indian spiritual activist (1869-1948)

"Had the doctrines of Jesus been preached always as pure as they came from his lips, the whole civilized world would now have been Christians."

– Thomas Jefferson,
3rd president of the United States (1743-1826)

*C**onsciousness exists in a range of vibrations, from the lowest (which is fear) to the highest (perfect love). And we come to earth to experience negativity so we can push against it and thereby raise our personal consciousness vibrations.* According to both the not-really-dead and spiritual sources as disparate as eastern religions and the Lord's Gospel teachings, this is the core reality of human life. And spiritual growth turns out to be an almost mechanical process, in that if you consistently do what will raise your spiritual vibrations away from fear and toward love, you are going to achieve real spiritual growth. We will discuss this process further in Chapters Seven through Nine.

So the wonderful news is that for the first time in human history we can be sure that spiritual growth is the reason why we enter bodies, and probably the whole reason why this universe exists; and even now we are beginning to understand how our spiritual development happens. But the bad news is that we also have learned that religious practice makes spiritual growth much more difficult. In fact, being very religious makes it almost impossible for us to grow spiritually at all! The irony is that we long have considered religions to be the province of spirituality. *But that was then.* We know much better now.

Christian Religious Practice is Spiritually Counterproductive

Here is why the ongoing practice of Christianity – and really of any traditional religion – will be an impediment to your spiritual growth:

- *Beliefs that are not based in facts are superstitions.* We hear the word "superstition" negatively, but its dictionary definition boils down to "an irrational belief." And we hear the word "faith" positively, but it means just "a belief in something for which there is no proof." So the words are synonyms. And no matter how Christians might celebrate their faith, the plain fact is that every Christian belief is based in teachings many hundreds of years old that are founded in the non-Gospels parts of the Bible, and in the unsupported teachings of fallible people who are now long dead.

- *Christian superstitions are grounded in fear.* When there is no evidence for a belief beyond the fact that people believed it long ago, it must be supported by something more if we hope to have it taken seriously. For religions, the easiest added motivator is fear. Fear of God's judgment, fear of hell, fear of negative outcomes: there are many sources of fear in Christianity!

- *Fear of God is the core Christian fear.* It is impossible for Christians not to fear a God that is presented to us as arbitrary, judgmental, quick to anger, and unable to forgive us for Adam's sin without the blood-sacrifice of God's own Son. If God is so wrathful as to be capable of requiring the sacrifice to Himself of His Own Child, then who knows what God might do to me? Fear of God is even seen as a virtue in Christianity, as if fear might be our best source of reverence. But since fear and love are polar opposites, it is impossible for you to love what you fear. So for us to fear God makes our ever genuinely loving God become flat-out impossible.

- *The superstitious fears that Christianity fosters create separations between people.* Those forty-two-thousand-odd Christian denominations are self-righteously separate from one another, and also separate from everyone who is not a Christian. As will be further discussed in later chapters, these ghastly artificial differences between people based upon differences in religious beliefs are anathema to spiritual growth. In fact, every human mind is inextricably part of the one eternal Mind that continuously manifests everything that we perceive to be real. So anything that comes between the minds of people is furthering the negative consciousness energy that is what Jesus came to earth to put behind us. The farther I advance from my old Christian practice, the more I come to see this division of the very Mind of God as the core Christian evil. If Christians were fighting over anything real – over interpretations of the Gospel teachings, perhaps – then their many divisions would at least be understandable! But in fact, Christians are battling over miniscule interpretations of nothing but superstitious fears. Sadly, the deeply splintered structure of modern-day Christianity is part of the reason why our present religious practice is anathema to spiritual growth.

- *Since Christianity as it is currently practiced is a collection of fear-based and divisive superstitions, it is little wonder that so many devout Christians are judgmental, unloving, and self-satisfied.* For any spiritual practice, the proof is in the pudding. And the most common complaint that people make about devout Christians is that they exhibit to an unusual degree the very personality traits that Jesus decried.

What is more, when I was a zealous Christian, I thought precisely as so many practicing Christians do now. I felt superior to people who didn't go to church. I was obeying every one of the Ten Commandments and giving God lots of my time and zeal, and I was quick to judge people who weren't meeting those standards. Having left traditional Christianity behind, I am now on the receiving end of all that Christian self-righteous judgment and disdain.

It is impossible to overstate the seriousness of this problem. Once you believe with all your heart that God will condemn you to hell unless you do specific things, but on the other hand if you will do those things then you are for sure going to heaven, then you have staked your well-being on an illusory and fear-based reality that is reinforced whenever you go to church. Oh, I do know how it feels! I was there for most of my life. Christian beliefs are both the cause and the cure of a fear so deep that the more firmly you believe, the more desperate you are to do whatever might buy you relief from that fear.

And yet, when they are objectively considered, all of our Christian fears are nonsense. Try telling someone who didn't grow up in Christianity that God is infinite love, but God also cannot forgive us for Adam's sin unless God gets to watch the murder of God's own Son. God is infinite love, but some of the people God created are the Elect, while other people that God created are from birth despised by God and forever damned. God is infinite love, but if we choose the wrong Christian denomination from among those forty-two thousand options, then we can kiss the thought of heaven goodbye.

Christianity Ignores Our Need for Spiritual Growth

Compounding Christianity's terrible problem with fear is the fact that no Christian denomination makes spiritual growth a priority. I was a practicing Christian into my fifties, and I even majored in Christianity in college, but I cannot recall ever being told how important spiritual growth really is, nor even what spiritual growth might be! What I was taught was that accepting Jesus as my savior and obeying the Christian rules was all I had to do to be a good Christian. Also going to church every Sunday. Plus putting a ten and not a five in the plate. Even the glorious teachings in those four Gospels never came up except as suggestions and aspirations.

In sum, all forms of modern Christianity instill in us a superstitious fear of God for which strict Christian practice is the only cure. We need to know no more than that to be certain that Christianity as we practice it now is anathema to Master Jesus. And it is a rejection of the one true God.

I understand how painful this chapter has been to read. I understand, too, that if you are deeply Christian, it probably inspired repeated bouts of fear as you wondered if your even having read these words might have imperiled your eternal soul.

My first book in this series was **The Fun of Dying,** *published in August of 2010, which contained the same Appendix IV that you will find here.* Over the course of the summer before that book was published, I became increasingly anguished about the possibility that my revealing what I had learned about the teachings of Jesus might be against the will of God, until finally one night I got down on my knees and sincerely prayed with all that was in me that if what was in that Appendix was not meant to see the light of day, then please, God, take me now! I promised God that my death would kill the book; I even gave my publisher that direction. I recall to this day my surprise when I woke up the next morning, still alive. It was only more than four years later – when my primary spirit guide came out to me through a medium – that I began to learn the extent to which God now wants these truths to be broadly known.

Please begin to think of spiritual growth not as something that happens mostly on Sundays, but rather as a way of living that permeates every aspect of your life, and transforms everything that you think and do in ways that are more profound and joyous than you even can imagine now. *Growing spiritually means a richer and more abundant life, both now and forevermore.*

CHAPTER FIVE
NO PRIMARY CHRISTIAN BELIEF IS BASED IN THE GOSPELS

"To judge from the notions expounded by theologians, one must conclude that God created most men simply with a view to crowding hell."

– Marquis de Sade, French nobleman, politician, philosopher, and writer (1740-1814)

"I cannot imagine a God who rewards and punishes the objects of his creation and is but a reflection of human frailty."

– Albert Einstein, German-born winner of the 1921 Nobel Prize in Physics (1879-1955)

"I think people often come to the synagogue, mosque, the church looking for God, and what we give them is religion."

– Gene Robinson, former Bishop of the Episcopal Diocese of New Hampshire

"Religion is no more the parent of morality than an incubator is the mother of a chicken."

– Lemuel K. Washburn, American free-thought writer (1846-1927)

"If Jesus had been killed twenty years ago, Catholic school children would be wearing little electric chairs around their necks instead of crosses."

– Lenny Bruce, Jewish-American stand-up comedian and social critic (1925-1966)

"Question with boldness even the existence of a God; because, if there be one, he must more approve of the homage of reason, then that of blindfolded fear."

– Thomas Jefferson, 3rd president of the United States (1743-1826)

*G*iven the perfect eternal truths that were brought to us by Jesus in the Gospels, it is astonishing to look at modern Christianity and realize that all its primary tenets are fear-based superstitions that contradict and even negate those very same Gospel teachings! I will go into this problem in more detail in Appendix V, so here I will just touch on a few of the worst of these false Christian beliefs.

For Jesus to Speak Against Judaism Was a Capital Crime

Before we begin, we must again acknowledge the fact that Jesus could not have spoken plainly. He was trying to move humankind past religions and teach us to relate to God directly, but for Him to have contradicted the prevailing religion of Judaism would have brought His execution. It is impossible to read the Gospels now with any level of understanding unless this fact is kept foremost in mind. And when we do read the Gospels with this understanding, we cannot help but admire the cleverness with which Jesus accomplished His task:

- He would share bits of a truth over days of time, knowing that the Temple guards who stalked Him would change so frequently that they wouldn't be able to put it all together. His followers, though, were constant, so they would hear and could process the entire truth. For example, He couldn't say flat-out that each of us will be our own afterlife judge, but over days he let us know first that God does not judge us, but has entrusted all judgment to the Son; then that the Son does not judge us either; and then that in fact the way we judge others will be the way that we will judge ourselves. He said, **"For not even the Father judges anyone, but He has given all judgment to the Son, so that all will honor the Son even as they honor the Father"** (JN 5:22-23). Then, **"If anyone hears My sayings and does not keep them, I do not judge him; for I did not come to judge the world, but to save the world"** (JN 12:47). And finally, **"Do not judge so that you will not be judged. For in the way you judge, you will be judged; and by your standard of measure, it will be measured to you"** (MT 7:1-2). As He plainly says, you will indeed be your own afterlife judge!

- He would affirm a Jewish belief, then add to it a truth that could transform our understanding of that belief. For example, when He was asked what was the greatest commandment, He didn't name any of the Ten Commandments. Instead, He replaced them all by saying, **"'You shall love the Lord your God with all your heart, and with all your soul, and with all your mind.' This is the great and foremost commandment. The second is like it, 'You shall love your neighbor as yourself.' On these two commandments depend the whole Law and the Prophets"** (MT 22:37-40). "The Law and the Prophets" was what the Jews of His day called our entire Old Testament. The Temple guards likely thought He was celebrating the Law and the Prophets, but we moderns are sophisticated enough to see that what He was doing was replacing all of ancient Jewish scripture with God's new law of perfect love.

- He couldn't say that God is infinitely creative and infinitely loving consciousness, and God is all that exists, but He could add a new aspect to the Jewish God, call it Spirit, and urge us to relate to God directly. Sadly, though, since He couldn't come right out and say that the cranky anthropomorphic God does not exist, early Christians kept that flawed God and added to it the Son and the Holy Spirit to create a trinity, which was a view of God that was fashionable in other religions of the day (for example, the Egyptian Osiris, Isis, and Horus). But God is not a trinity, since that image implies that God is divided! No, the only God is infinitely creative and infinitely loving Spirit. Yet again, Jesus is perfectly right.

- Sometimes Jesus would speak via His actions. He dined with prostitutes and tax collectors, and as He walked through a field on the Sabbath Day He harvested heads from some of the standing grain. Only when He was asked by His followers why He was doing these forbidden things did He give them the meanings of His actions.

- He often told parables, little stories that had deeper meanings, and then He might say, **"He who has ears to hear, let him hear."** You can almost see the Lord winking!

Appendix IV explores this issue in more detail. But unless you read the Gospels with the constant awareness that Jesus cannot speak plainly so He is relying on us to seek His deeper meanings, you never will understand the Gospel words. To this day, Jesus implores us to dig deeper! He said, **"So I say to you, ask, and it** will be given to you; seek, and you will find; knock, and it will be opened to you. For everyone who asks, receives; and he who seeks, finds; and to him who knocks, it will be opened" (LK 11:9-10).

The Three Most Fear-Based False Christian Beliefs

Among the forty-two-thousand-odd modern Christian denominations, there is considerable variation in what is taught, but here are three core sets of erroneous beliefs that pretty much all Christian denominations share. Each of them is a highly destructive and anti-Gospels, fear-based superstition.

Substitutionary Atonement

The Christian doctrine of substitutionary atonement – or sacrificial redemption, if you prefer – is contrary to the Gospel teachings. And it paints a terrible picture of God, while it also humiliates Jesus! To accept this teaching as it is commonly understood requires us to believe that God is so petty and judgmental that God cannot forgive us for Adam's sin – in plain words, God cannot forgive us for being human – unless God gets to watch the murder of God's only begotten Son. We must further believe that Jesus came to us primarily as a sacrificial Lamb, and nothing He says in the Gospels should be seen as more than mere suggestions because it is only His sacrificial death that "saves" us. *He didn't actually need to say a word!*

To be frank, this didn't make sense to me even when I was deeply Catholic, but whenever I asked a priest about it, he told me it was "a sacred mystery." But everything about this idea is horrendous and insulting to the only God! We will elaborate further in Appendix V, but for now please just try to put yourself in God's shoes. Imagine that your children have made a mess of the living room. Do you say, "Well, kids will be kids," and get the vacuum? Or do you ponder which of your children you would prefer to watch being horribly murdered so you can feel better about forgiving the others? If that image horrifies you – and it should! – then ask yourself this question: how is it possible that you are more loving and more forgiving than the only God? *(Quick word to the wise: you're not.)*

End-Times Beliefs

Many Christians believe that at some point a wrathful Jesus will come back to rescue the Just, and will cast the Unjust into eternal fire. These beliefs are so widely held that such related theories as the Rapture have become nearly mainstream. *But to be blunt, anyone who believes in end-times theology has not the least understanding of the Lord's mission or His Gospel message.*

Here are His mission and His message in one sentence: **Jesus came to teach us how to raise our personal consciousness vibrations, and thereby raise the collective vibrations of all of humankind away from fear and toward more perfect love so we can bring the Kingdom of God on earth.** He makes all of this perfectly clear in the Gospels, so we don't even need further elaboration from the dead. And for Jesus to act as the Book of Revelation has Him acting would infuse humankind with massive fear, and would negate the whole purpose of His Gospel teachings. Are we to believe that a Being so elevated that He literally came to us as God on earth came to bring to us the most perfect set of spiritual teachings humankind ever has received; and then just a few decades after His death, He said, "Oh never mind," and He decided instead to destroy humankind in a fear-drenched war?

Not surprisingly, the not-really-dead confirm that there can never be an end-times war. The Biblical Book of Revelation was part of a genre of revenge-literature that was created during a time of terrible Christian persecution. Of course they would have wanted to be rescued this way! But that book is only a terrible fantasy tied to a particular time and place. *It has nothing to do with Jesus or with the genuine God.*

Sin

The very concept of "sin" is counter-productive! Anything that makes people fearful is antithetical to the Gospel teachings, which is why Jesus does away with the Ten Commandments and all the other Jewish laws in the Gospels and replaces them with God's law of love. Not only does He tell us that the entire Old Testament is outmoded, but He pointedly breaks the Jewish Sabbath laws. He even performs healings on the Sabbath. When His followers challenge Him, He says, **"The Sabbath was made for man, and not man for the Sabbath"** (MK 2:27). He even tells us, **"The Son of Man is Lord of the Sabbath"** (MT 12:8). This is pretty radical stuff! But it is important, since when people are focusing on the arbitrary and fear-based laws of man, they cannot sufficiently free their minds to concentrate on the perfect truths of God.

When you take away sin, Armageddon, and substitutionary atonement, what aspects of modern Christianity are left? Not much. That old wrapper of Christian superstitions in which the church-builders packaged the Gospel teachings now lies in tatters at our feet. And actually, that is wonderful news! We have spent the past two thousand years distracted by that packaging, loving it, serving it, and forgetting that it was only a wrapper. It is time for us now joyously to turn to Jesus alone as we open God's perfect gift and gladly toss away that old wrapping. The Lord has waited for us long enough! As He says, **"If you hold to my teaching, you are really my disciples. Then you will know the truth, and the truth will set you free"** (JN 8:31-32).

The Joy Of Really

Following Jesus

CHAPTER SIX
JESUS MEANT TO START A MOVEMENT, NOT A RELIGION

"Any religion that professes to be concerned about the souls of men and is not concerned about the slums that damn them, the economic conditions that strangle them and the social conditions that cripple them is a spiritually moribund religion awaiting burial."

– Martin Luther King, Jr.,
Winner of the 1964 Nobel Peace Prize (1929-1968)

"An error does not become truth by reason of multiplied propagation, nor does truth become error because nobody sees it. Truth stands, even if there be no public support. It is self-sustained."

– Mahatma Gandhi,
Indian spiritual activist (1869-1948)

"A new idea is first condemned as ridiculous and then dismissed as trivial, until finally, it becomes what everybody knows."

– William James,
American philosopher and psychologist (1842-1910)

"To me, religion is an agreement between a group of people about what God is. Spirituality is a one-on-one relationship."

– Steve Earle, American rock,
country and folk singer-songwriter, author, and actor

"If there is a God, atheism must seem to Him as less of an insult than religion."

– Edmond de Goncourt, French writer,
literary critic, art critic, publisher (1822-1896)

"The main object of religion is not to get a man into heaven, but to get heaven into him."

– Thomas Hardy,
English novelist and poet (1840-1928)

"To the corruptions of Christianity I am indeed opposed; but not to the genuine precepts of Jesus himself. I am a Christian, in the only sense he wished any one to be; sincerely attached to his doctrines, in preference to all others; ascribing to himself every human excellence; & believing he never claimed any other."

– Thomas Jefferson,
3rd president of the United States (1743-1826)

*I*f you have read this far, you have seen good evidence that the Christianity that we still practice now must be the biggest "whoops" in history. By which I do not mean to say that God has ever been upset or fooled. Despite what scientists believe, in fact human beings have free will, and that free will turns out to be an essential element as we work to achieve our own spiritual growth. How can we choose love in every instance unless we also have the power and the right to choose fear, hatred, and all the other low-vibration emotions? That fallible men have ignored the central importance of the Gospel teachings of Jesus, and have instead built around them what became just one more sadly fear-based religion, has only delayed the moment when those perfect teachings can at last become a central force in every human life. From an eternal perspective, what is two thousand years?

Jesus tells us in the Gospels that His purpose in coming was to teach us some essential truths, and to help us to get beyond religions so we can relate directly to the genuine God. He says all of this so plainly that the more you read the Gospels, the more you marvel at the thickness of all those twenty centuries of Christian leaders! How could they have clung to their makeshift religion in the face of such perfect divine wisdom?

Jesus Meant to Start a Secular Spiritual Movement

Let's look here briefly at how we know that Jesus did not intend to start any religion, and certainly He never meant to give us the religion that now bears His name. Even through those early decades when His teachings were passed down orally, through two translations from Aramaic into Greek and then from Greek into English, and through the long centuries when the Catholic Church had exclusive custody of the Gospels so it could have edited them to say whatever it liked, the Lord's determination to get us past mere religious beliefs and help us learn the perfect truth of God remains both powerful and endearing. For example:

- *Jesus told us not to package His teachings with any others. He insisted that we keep them separate.* Many Christians can quote this famous passage, but they seem never to focus on its meaning! How can we interpret it to mean anything other than a plea from the Lord that we keep His teachings separate from the prevailing religion? **"But no one puts a patch of unshrunk cloth on an old garment; for the patch pulls away from the garment, and a worse tear results. Nor do people put new wine into old wineskins; otherwise the wineskins burst, and the wine pours out and the wineskins are ruined; but they put new wine into fresh wineskins, and both are preserved"** (MT 9:16-17). He expects that some teachers of the old Jewish law will latch onto what He is saying, but even these clergymen are directed to keep His teachings separate from their religious practice. **"Therefore every scribe who has become a disciple of the kingdom of heaven is like a head of a household, who brings out of his treasure things new and old"** (MT 13:52).

- *There is Gospel evidence that Jesus means His teachings actually to replace Judaism.* For example, initially He sent his disciples only to Jews, whom He called "the lost sheep of Israel." "These twelve Jesus sent out after instructing them: **'Do not go in the way of the Gentiles, and do not enter any city of the**

Samaritans; but rather go to the lost sheep of the house of Israel. And as you go, preach, saying, 'The kingdom of heaven is at hand'" (MT 10:5-7). He said, "The Law and the Prophets (what the Jews of the day called the modern Old Testament) were proclaimed until John (the Baptist); since that time the gospel of the kingdom of God has been preached" (LK 16:16). When you read the words of Jesus with an open mind, it seems clear that He wanted first to free the Jews from their old fear-based religion, and then to make of them God's ambassadors for truth to all the other nations. It was only when He received a warmer reception from Samaritans and some others than whatever He got from the Jews of His day that He began to teach these non-Jews as well.

- *Jesus seems to have despised religious leaders and clergymen.* Back when I was a devout Christian, I would wince to read some of these passages! For example, He said, **"Beware of the scribes who like to walk around in long robes, and like respectful greetings in the market places, and chief seats in the synagogues and places of honor at banquets, who devour widows' houses, and for appearance's sake offer long prayers; these will receive greater condemnation"** (MK 12:38-40).

- *Jesus was bothered to find that a religion was already being built around Him.* He said, **"Why do you call me 'Lord, Lord,' and do not do what I say?"** (LK 6:46). **"Not everyone who says to me, 'Lord, Lord,' will enter the kingdom of heaven, but only he who does the will**

of my Father who is in heaven will enter" (MT 7:21). He never wanted personal worship. For Him, it was only His teachings that mattered.

- *He was especially bothered that the clergymen of His day continued to preach their old fear-based religion.* They did this, even while His teachings about love and forgiveness and how to enter the kingdom of God were being ignored. He said, **"Woe to you religious lawyers! For you have taken away the key of knowledge; you yourselves did not enter, and you hindered those who were entering"** (LK 11:52). **"But woe to you, scribes and Pharisees, hypocrites, because you shut off the kingdom of heaven from people; for you do not enter in yourselves, nor do you allow those who are entering to go in"** (MT 23:13).

- *Jesus considered practicing the religion of His day to be a barrier to true spiritual practice.* In this, He echoed the complaint of the greatest Old Testament prophet. He said, **"Why do you transgress the commandment of God for the sake of your tradition?... You hypocrites! Rightly did Isaiah prophesy of you: 'This people honors me with their lips, but their hearts are far away from me. But in vain do they worship me, teaching as doctrines the precepts of men'"** (MT 15:3-9). And He said, **"Neglecting the commandment of God, you hold to the tradition of men... You are experts at setting aside the commandment of God in order to keep your tradition"** (MK 7:8-9). It is hard not to feel His frustration as He tries to open people's eyes and rescue them from all fear-based religions. How could anyone imagine that a man who says these things would want to start yet one more fear-based religion? His own words leave no doubt that was the last thing that He wanted.

- *The word "church" appears just twice in the Gospels, and neither mention came from Jesus.* Of course, every mention of the word "church" during the Lord's lifetime would have been an anachronism, since no religion claiming to be based on His teachings existed until after His death. These two mentions occur close to one another in the Book of Matthew, and it is laughably easy to see that they were added much later. **"I also say to you that you are Peter, and upon this rock I will build My church; and the gates of Hades will not overpower it. I will give you the keys of the kingdom of heaven; and whatever you bind on earth shall have been bound in heaven, and whatever you loose on earth shall have been loosed in heaven"** (MT 16:18-19). And **"If your brother sins, go and show him his fault in private; if he listens to you, you have won your brother. But if he does not listen to you, take one or two more with you, so that by the mouth of two or three witnesses every fact may be confirmed. If he refuses to listen to them, tell it to the church; and if he refuses to listen even to the church, let him be to you as a Gentile and a tax collector. Truly I say to you, whatever you bind on earth shall have been bound in heaven; and whatever you loose on earth shall have been loosed in heaven"** (MT 18:15-18). Oh, where to begin? Note first that His having been quoted as saying that Peter is the "rock" on which He will build His church is a pun in Greek, but Jesus spoke Aramaic. Note, too, that references to "the keys to the kingdom of heaven" and "the gates of Hades" would have been foreign to the Jesus of the Gospels, as would have been the legalistic process outlined in the second quotation. And the idea that a living human being could "bind" God to anything would have been anathema to the Lord! That talk of shunning tax collectors? Jesus made a point of dining with tax collectors and other social dregs. All of this comes from a later time, when Christians were building a law-based religion headed by a Pope. Not only did Jesus not say these things, but clearly those who much later wrote them down hadn't even closely read the Gospels.

- *Jesus tells us that public prayer is hypocrisy, and He urges us to speak to God in private.* What stronger evidence could there be that the Lord was trying to rescue us from practicing a religion, and instead He was teaching us to relate to God on our own? For example, He said, **"When you pray, you are not to be like the hypocrites; for they love to stand and pray in the synagogues and on the street corners so that they may be seen by men. Truly I say to you, they have their reward in full. But you, when you pray, go into your inner room, close your door and pray to your Father who is in secret, and your Father who sees what is done in secret will reward you"** (MT 6:5-6). All of this is consistent with the Lord's Gospel teaching that God is loving Spirit, and with His wish to teach us

to relate to God directly. But it is nothing that He ever
would have said if He had meant to start His own
religion.

- *He urges us to follow His teachings strictly, but never
does He tell us His teachings are meant to be part of
any religion.* Instead, He says things like, **"But go and
learn what this means: 'I desire mercy, not sacrifice'"**
(MT 9:13) and, **"If you hold to my teaching, you are
really my disciples. Then you will know the truth,
and the truth will set you free"** (JN 8:31-32).

- *He tries repeatedly to replace the old Jewish God with
the genuine God, which is Spirit, and to tell us that
Spirit is within us.* To speak against the Jewish God
was during His lifetime a capital crime, but this point
was so essential to Him that He came back to it often.
He said, **"God is Spirit, and those who worship Him
must worship in spirit and in truth"** (JN 4:24). And,
**"It is the Spirit who gives life; the flesh profits
nothing; the words that I have spoken to you are
spirit and are life"** (JN 6:63). **"If you love me, you will
keep my commandments. I will ask the Father, and
He will give you another Helper, that He may be with
you forever; that is the Spirit of truth, whom the
world cannot receive, because it does not see Him or
know Him, but you know Him because He abides
with you and will be in you"** (JN 14:15-17). Christians
have used this last quotation as a basis for their Trinity
doctrine, but since Jesus never spoke of a Trinity, it is
more likely that He said it this way to make certain that
people trapped in the old religion would nevertheless

know that God can relate to us directly as Spirit, even though the laws of the day made it hard for Him to come right out and tell people that actually God *is* Spirit.

- *What is always important to Jesus is not religious beliefs, but His own Gospel teachings!* For example, He says, **"Therefore everyone who hears these words of Mine and acts on them may be compared to a wise man who built his house on the rock. And the rain fell, and the floods came, and the winds blew and slammed against that house; and yet it did not fall, for it had been founded on the rock. Everyone who hears these words of Mine and does not act on them, will be like a foolish man who built his house on the sand. The rain fell, and the floods came, and the winds blew and slammed against that house; and it fell— and great was its fall"** (MT 7:24-27). Christianity as it has been practiced for more than fifteen hundred years does not take the Gospel teachings of Jesus nearly as seriously as He means them to be taken. Christians have heard those words and not acted on them. Christianity has been built on sand, so as Jesus predicted, now it is falling. *And in the twenty-first century, great indeed is its fall!*

- *Jesus repeatedly talks about His teachings not as a new religion, but instead as important information to be disseminated to all nations.* As He gathers His first followers, He says to them the like of, **"Follow Me, and I will make you fishers of men"** (MT 4:19). He is making that call to many of us today. This core charge that we use the teachings of Jesus to enlighten the world is apparent in what is commonly called the Great Commission: **"All authority has been given to Me in heaven and on earth. Go therefore and make disciples of all the nations… teaching them to observe all that I commanded you; and lo, I am with you always, even to the end of the age"** (MT 28:19-20). He doesn't tell them to set up churches, does He? No, He tells them to teach, and to make new disciples who can join them in spreading these essential truths to everyone on the face of the earth.

It Is Up to Us to Give to the Lord the Movement That He Wanted

For those who love Jesus, the choice that He is giving to us now is clear. He plainly tells us in the Gospels that the religion that bears His name is not based on His teachings. In fact, it is anathema to the work that He came to do! And now it acts as an active barrier to the Lord's charge that we proclaim God's truth to the world. *For the Lord's sake, it is time for us to break free of that false old-time religion.* We know that the pioneers in preaching God's truth in the face of so many untruths will have trials ahead, but we also will be among the first true followers of Jesus. And that will be joyous! As He says, **"Come to Me, all who are weary and heavy-laden, and I will give you rest. Take My yoke upon you and learn from Me, for I am gentle and humble in heart, and you will find rest for your souls. For My yoke is easy and My burden is light"** (MT 11:28-30).

CHAPTER SEVEN
BRINGING THE KINGDOM OF GOD ON EARTH

"Be the Change That You Wish to See in the World."
— Mahatma Gandhi,
Indian spiritual activist (1869-1948)

"The mind is everything. What you think you become."
— Gautama Buddha, Nepalese-Indian sage,
(563 BCE/480 BCE-c.483 BCE/400 BCE)

"I think there's every reason this 21st century will be much happier."
— 14th Dalai Lama, Tibetan Monk

"The God who existed before any religion counts on you to make the oneness of the human family known and celebrated."
— Desmond Tutu, South African Anglican cleric
and theologian (1931-2021)

"Man cannot discover new oceans unless he has the courage to lose sight of the shore."
— Andre Gide, French winner of the
1947 Nobel Prize in Literature (1869-1951)

"Minds are like parachutes. They only function when they are opened."
— Lord Thomas Dewar,
Scottish whiskey distiller (1864-1930)

"Upon the altar of God I have sworn eternal hostility against every form of tyranny over the mind of man."
— Thomas Jefferson,
3rd president of the United States (1743-1826)

When you read the four canonical Gospels straight through, you cannot avoid concluding that what Jesus came to do was to bring what He called the kingdom of God on earth. He mentions the kingdom of Heaven more than thirty times in the Book of Matthew, and the kingdom of God four times in Matthew, fourteen times in Mark, and more than thirty times in Luke. These three books share common roots. And they differ significantly from John, where the kingdom of God comes up just twice; but no one reading the four Gospels together can have any doubt that bringing God's Kingdom to earth is the Lord's obsession.

Defining the Kingdom of God

What may be more difficult to puzzle out is just what He means by these two kingdom terms. At one time I differentiated between them, thinking that one might refer to the Summerland areas that we first enter at death, and perhaps the other was a reference to the highest levels of the afterlife; but for a number of reasons I have come to think that both terms mean the same thing. They refer to the joyously blissful, love-based higher levels of the afterlife, which can be attained only by those who are more spiritually advanced. **And what Jesus came to earth to do was to make this anger- and hatred- and fear-filled planet into a love-filled mimic of those highest heavens.**

To make that even possible, He first replaced the entire Old Testament – what was then called "the Law and the Prophets" – with "the gospel of the kingdom of God." The "John" that He refers to here is John the Baptist. He said, **"The Law and the Prophets were proclaimed until John; since that time the gospel of the kingdom of God has been preached, and everyone is forcing his**

way into it" (LK 16:16). What Jesus means by saying that "everyone is forcing his way into it" is unclear, but it seems to be a kind of salesman's pitch, a reference to the size of the crowds that had begun to follow Him.

And here is the moment – the most important moment in all four Gospels – where He defines for us "the gospel of the Kingdom of God." When someone asked Jesus what was the most important commandment, He didn't name any of the Ten Commandments. Instead He said, **"'You shall love the Lord your God with all your heart, and with all your soul, and with all your mind.' This is the great and foremost commandment. The second is like it, 'You shall love your neighbor as yourself.' On these two commandments depend the whole Law and the Prophets"** (MT 22:37-40). With these words He replaced our entire Old Testament with God's law of love, and then He proceeded to spend His entire ministry sharing with us the easiest method for raising our consciousness vibration away from fear and toward more perfect love that ever has been given to us (please recall Chapter Two).

How We Can Achieve the Kingdom of God

When we understand that the kingdom of God refers to the spiritual perfection of the highest afterlife levels, and that the stated mission of Jesus is to bring this level of spiritual perfection to all the earth, we can easily see that some of His Gospel references are to our efforts to attain the higher afterlife levels for ourselves, while others refer to the process of bringing that level of spiritual perfection to our lives on earth.

Here are some examples of how Jesus tells his followers that their individual task is to grow spiritually, and just saying the right words or practicing some particular religion is not enough:

"Why do you call me 'Lord, Lord,' and do not do what I say?" (LK 6:46)

"Not everyone who says to me, 'Lord, Lord,' will enter the kingdom of heaven, but only he who does the will of my Father who is in heaven will enter" (MT 7:21).

"If you hold to my teaching, you are really my disciples. Then you will know the truth, and the truth will set you free" (JN 8:31-32).

"Truly I say to you that the tax collectors and prostitutes will get into the kingdom of God before you. For John came to you in the way of righteousness and you did not believe him; but the tax collectors and prostitutes did believe him; and you, seeing this, did not even feel remorse afterward so as to believe him" (MT 21:31-32). The John referred to here is itinerant preacher John the Baptist, who first baptized Jesus as the Lord began His ministry.

For Jesus it was spiritual growth that was important. He said emphatically, **"I say to you that many will come from east and west, and recline at the table with Abraham, Isaac and Jacob in the kingdom of heaven; but the sons of the kingdom will be cast out into the outer darkness; in that place there will be weeping and gnashing of teeth"** (MT 8:11-13).

This last reference is astonishing! Those that we used to think were dead tell us consistently that there is no fiery hell, but the lowest afterlife levels are exactly as Jesus describes them here: they are a cold and smelly outer darkness full of wailing demons who actually are just people gone very wrong spiritually. And Jesus knew that. He accurately described it. Let that further little nugget of truth sink in!

Jesus tells us that spiritual growth is harder if we allow anything other than our spiritual growth to be more important to us. He says, **"I say to you, it is easier for a camel to go through the eye of a needle, than for a rich man to enter the kingdom of God"** (MT 19:24). This is not as bad as it sounds. In Jesus's day, there was a narrow gate into Jerusalem called "the Eye of the Needle" that pack-camels were too wide to pass through unless they first were unloaded. It has been suggested that this was the Lord's way of saying that to enter the kingdom of God you must shed your attachment to wealth. Even normal life cannot be allowed to be more important to us than working to raise our own spiritual vibration and working to spread the kingdom of God on earth. For example, someone He had called to join Him said, "'Lord, permit me first to go and bury my father.' But Jesus said to him, **'Allow the dead to bury their own dead; but as for you, go and proclaim everywhere the kingdom of God'"** (LK 9:59-60).

Jesus uses the spiritual purity of children as exemplars of what we all are striving to attain. When His disciples tried to keep children from bothering Him, He would say the like of, **"Permit the children to come to Me, and do not hinder them, for the kingdom of God belongs to such as these. Truly I say to you, whoever does not receive the kingdom of God like a child will not enter it at all"** (LK 18:16-17). I have by now met a number of people on earth who are spiritually quite advanced, and I can tell you that even in old age they are indeed surprisingly childlike, sweet and loving, and eventually unable even to be near people who are fearful, angry, or otherwise negative.

Jesus Said the Kingdom of God on Earth Would Begin in His Own Day

Jesus appears to have told us that His brief ministry was going to bring the kingdom of God to earth within the lifetimes of some of His followers. For example, He said, **"The time is fulfilled, and the kingdom of God is at hand; repent and believe in the gospel"** (MK 1:15). And He said, **"But I say to you truthfully, there are some of those standing here who will not taste death until they see the kingdom of God"** (LK 9:27).

But He also told us that this transformation of the world from a place of fear to a place of love would be a gradual process. "Now having been questioned by the Pharisees as to when the kingdom of God was coming, He answered them and said, **'The kingdom of God is not coming with signs to be observed; nor will they say, "Look, here it is!" or, "There it is!" For behold, the kingdom of God is in your midst'"** (LK 17:20-21). In some translations He says the kingdom of God is "among you" or "within you." Some commentators believe He is telling us that God's Kingdom really is internal, but after checking a number of modern translations I have come to think that what He is saying is that the Kingdom is already appearing on earth in His lifetime, and its triumph will be a gradual process.

Further supporting this idea is the way Jesus stresses the Kingdom's small beginnings and rapid growth. He would say the like of, **"What is the kingdom of God like, and to what shall I compare it? It is like a mustard seed, which a man took and threw into his own garden; and it grew and became a tree, and the birds of the air nested in its branches."** And again He said, **"To what shall I compare the kingdom of God? It is like leaven, which a** woman took and hid in three pecks of flour until it was all leavened" (LK 13:18-21).

And Jesus's last charge to His disciples was that they begin right then to spread His teachings to all the earth. He said, **"All authority has been given to Me in heaven and on earth. Go therefore and make disciples of all the nations, … teaching them to observe all that I commanded you; and lo, I am with you always, even to the end of the age"** (MT 28 18-20).

For a long time I thought those building Christianity had horrifyingly subverted the Lord's work, and the religion had actively delayed the advent of the kingdom of God on earth by a further two millennia. Very recently, though, I have been given to understand in no uncertain terms that the past two thousand years have unfolded consistently with the will of God. Why this history has been what God intended is a discussion beyond the scope of this book, but we can know now with joy that all is unfolding as God has intended that it should unfold. And, wonderfully, ours is the generation in which the Lord's bringing of God's kingdom on earth is actively underway!

Reincarnation

Those that we used to think were dead tell us that each of us lives many earth-lives. Each lifetime is planned as something like a trip to a classroom, or to a spiritual gym, to give us lots of opportunities to encounter negativity so we can deal with its stresses and learn to choose love over negative emotions in every circumstance. Human life on earth is all about spiritual growth, and living repeated lifetimes apparently is the most effective way for us to grow spiritually. So reincarnation is a fact, but it is not remotely like religious versions of reincarnation. For one thing, since there is no objective time in the eternal levels where we plan our earth-lives, we don't necessarily plan our lives in earth-years order. And for another, because of the lack of objective time, apparently all our earth-lives are happening something like simultaneously.

So if reincarnation is a fact, then why did Jesus never talk about it? Actually, He did talk about it. I majored in Christian history in college, and even fifty years later I still recall the lecture about the Council of Nicaea, where we learned that as the Council had assembled the Christian Bible in 325, it had removed from the canonical Gospels every reference to reincarnation that it could find "because they worried that if people thought they could keep coming back, they wouldn't try hard enough the first time." That was the reason why they took scissors to what they were insisting as they assembled their Bible was "the inspired word of God."

So whatever Jesus may have said about reincarnation, very little of it remains. *And what does remain has been imbued with religious meanings the Lord clearly never intended.* Here is the best example of this travesty:

"Now there was a man of the Pharisees, named Nicodemus, a ruler of the Jews; this man came to Jesus by night and said to Him, 'Rabbi, we know that You have come from God as a teacher; for no one can do these signs that You do unless God is with him.' Jesus answered and said to him, **'Truly, truly, I say to you, unless one is born again he cannot see the kingdom of God.'**

"Nicodemus said to Him, 'How can a man be born when he is old? He cannot enter a second time into his mother's womb and be born, can he?' Jesus answered, **'Truly, truly, I say to you, unless one is born of water and the Spirit he cannot enter into the kingdom of God. That which is born of the flesh is flesh, and** that which is born of the Spirit is spirit. Do not be amazed that I said to you, "You must be born again." The wind blows where it wishes and you hear the sound of it, but do not know where it comes from and where it is going; so is everyone who is born of the Spirit'" (JN 3:1-8).

Even after two thousand years and two translations, it is clear what Jesus is talking about here! A baby is both flesh and spirit, and it is born in a gush of water-like amniotic fluid. Those who are between lives and yet to be born again indeed are very much like the wind, invisible to those on earth and free to roam where they will.

The Christian interpretation of the term "born again" does not remotely fit these Gospel words. And it doesn't agree with what we are learning from those that we used to think were dead, who consistently tell us that whether or not we are baptized or we ever claim Jesus to be our savior – indeed, whether we practice any religion at all – everyone goes to the selfsame afterlife at death. No, this is a reference to reincarnation that was subtle enough that the Nicaean Councilors missed it.

Jesus tells us that in order for us to grow spiritually, we will need to live repeated lifetimes on earth. And in this, once again, He is precisely right.

Raising the Consciousness Vibration of This Planet

As was mentioned in Chapter Two, we are told that for at least the past century there has been an effort underway – orchestrated at the highest levels of reality – to raise the consciousness vibration of this planet away from fear and anger and toward ever more perfect love. In other words, **Jesus is right now working to bring the kingdom of God on earth.** He talked about its happening within the lifetimes of some of His earthly followers, and so indeed it might have happened if the religion-makers had not shut down the process by inventing fear-based Christianity and subsuming within it the Lord's Gospel words. Those that Jesus had called to go out and teach us how to bring the kingdom of God on earth were soon instead preaching substitutionary atonement and the notion that only Christians are "saved." An obvious question to ask is why Jesus didn't step in and correct Christianity a whole lot sooner than this; but as was said earlier in this chapter, I have lately been told from a very high level that this delay was deliberate. Since we can reincarnate out of order in a greater reality without time, those many years in which Christianity was erroneous and fear-based have now created nearly two millennia into which people can choose to incarnate in search of more rapid spiritual growth. And anyway, from the viewpoint of those at the highest vibrational levels, two thousand years is like an afternoon.

So we know that the process of bringing the kingdom of God on earth is underway now. And those of us who have studied the Gospel teachings are delighted to report that the way things are getting a whole lot worse was predicted by the Lord, and actually it is good news! Jesus told us that the advent of the kingdom of God on earth would be a time of great tribulation. He said, **"Brother will betray brother to death, and a father his child; and children will rise up against parents and cause them to be put to death"** (MT 10:20-21), **"(f)or those days will be a time of tribulation such as has not occurred since the beginning of the creation which God created until now, and never will"** (MK 13:19). So He predicted that our very attempts to turn humankind away from fear and toward love were going to cause the forces of negativity and fear to fight back, hard.

But still, we have no choice but to fight for the triumph of love over fear. Those at the highest levels tell us that the earth is so deeply negative now that without divine intervention, wars and disasters will proliferate, and humankind may not survive; so they are working through us to turn the tide. As Jesus said, **"These things I have spoken to you, so that in Me you may have peace. In the world you have tribulation, but take courage; I have overcome the world"** (JN 16:33). **"And lo, I am with you always, even to the end of the age"** (MT 28:20).

CHAPTER EIGHT
WHAT JESUS MEANS WHEN HE TALKS ABOUT FORGIVENESS

"If you are willing to look at another person's behavior toward you as a reflection of the state of their relationship with themselves rather than a statement of your value as a person, then you will, over a period of time cease to react at all."

– Yogi Bhajan, Pakistani yogi,
spiritual teacher and entrepreneur (1929-2004)

"Resentment is like drinking poison and then hoping it will kill your enemies."

– Nelson Mandela, South African political leader
and philanthropist (1918-2013)

"Forgiveness is the fragrance the violet sheds on the heel that has crushed it."

– Mark Twain, American writer,
entrepreneur, publisher, and lecturer (1835-1910)

"Forgiveness is not an occasional act, it is a constant ATTITUDE!"

– Martin Luther King, Jr.,
Winner of the 1964 Nobel Peace Prize (1929-1968)

"The weak can never forgive. Forgiveness is the attribute of the strong."

– Mahatma Gandhi,
Indian spiritual activist (1869-1948)

"All men are by nature equal, made all of the same earth by one Workman; and however we deceive ourselves, as dear unto God is the poor peasant as the mighty prince."

– Plato, Classical Greek
Philosopher (428/427 or 424/423-348/347 BC)

"The truth is, that the greatest enemies to the doctrines of Jesus are those, calling themselves the expositors of them, who have perverted them for the structure of a system of fancy absolutely incomprehensible, and without any foundation in His genuine words."

– Thomas Jefferson,
3rd president of the United States (1743-1826)

*T*he loss to humankind that lies in the fact that those who control the teachings of Jesus have for two thousand years refused to share them with the world is beyond all *calculation.* Imagine a world where for the past thousand years there have been no wars, no strife, no anger, no poor, and only ever more perfect love! Or even just imagine a world where everyone understands the purpose of human life, so we all can see that grubbing for money rather than loving and helping others will get us big demerits in the one school that counts.

The Gospel Teachings Are the Easiest Route to Rapid Spiritual Growth

Closely following the Gospel teachings begins a cycle of increasing peace and joy, and an exultant, ambient love in a life that is no longer troubled by fears, or even by any negative thought. Living the teachings is a particular happiness, not dependent on anything external. I was already old when I began to take the teachings of Jesus as seriously as He means them to be taken. But after just a few years of living them, my life has been so entirely transformed that I barely can recall the way I was before.

It is important that we understand the Gospel teachings on forgiveness and love as not just suggestions, but rather as a rapid and almost mechanical way to assist our minds in growing spiritually. ***In this effort the teachings must work together.*** It is spiritually of little value to pursue either forgiveness or love just on its own, since they give essential support to one another in elevating our consciousness vibrations.

And Jesus clearly understood that fact. This parable is long, but it is so central that it is worth quoting here in full:

"For it is just like a man about to go on a journey, who called his own slaves and entrusted his possessions to them. To one he gave five talents, to another, two, and to another, one, each according to his own ability; and he went on his journey. Immediately the one who had received the five talents went and traded with them, and gained five more talents. In the same manner the one who had received the two talents gained two more. But he who received the one talent went away, and dug a hole in the ground and hid his master's money.

"Now after a long time the master of those slaves came and settled accounts with them. The one who had received the five talents came up and brought five more talents, saying, 'Master, you entrusted five talents to me. See, I have gained five more talents.' His master said to him, 'Well done, good and faithful slave. You were faithful with a few things, I will put you in charge of many things; enter into the joy of your master.'

"Also the one who had received the two talents came up and said, 'Master, you entrusted two talents to me. See, I have gained two more talents.' His master said to him, 'Well done, good and faithful slave. You were faithful with a few things, I will put you in charge of many things; enter into the joy of your master.'

"And the one also who had received the one talent came up and said, 'Master, I knew you to be a hard man, reaping where you did not sow and gathering where you scattered no seed. And I was afraid, and went away and hid your talent in the ground. See, you have what is yours.'

"But his master answered and said to him, 'You wicked, lazy slave, you knew that I reap where I did not sow and gather where I scattered no seed. Then you ought to have put my money in the bank, and on my arrival I would have received my money back with interest. Therefore take away the talent from him, and give it to the one who has the ten talents.'

"For to everyone who has, more shall be given, and he will have an abundance; but from the one who does not have, even what he does have shall be taken away. Throw out the worthless slave into the outer darkness; in that place there will be weeping and gnashing of teeth'" (MT 25:14-30).

Jesus was talking to first-century primitives. He was trying to get across to them concepts that even many people in the twenty-first century have trouble grasping, and he hit upon an excellent analogy. *Growing spiritually is very much like the accomulation of earthly wealth.* It is of great value. It must be put to work in order to grow it. And if we don't grow it, we might lose it, since our spiritual status will not simply stay stable. We cannot know how often and in how many ways he might have used this analogy, but it is brilliant here. And it is important to understand that the risk is real! Jesus isn't threatening us, but rather He is stating a fact that is based in what we might see as consciousness physics. Either we progress spiritually or we regress, but we cannot stand still. Nor can we even hide our spiritual status. He says, **"For nothing is hidden that will not become evident, nor anything secret that will not be known and come to light. So take care how you listen; for whoever has, to him more shall be given; and whoever does not have, even what he thinks he has shall be taken away from him"** (LK 8:17-18).

This is a point worth emphasizing. We come to earth to grow spiritually, but since we have not understood that fact, many of us have spent our lives seeking earthly wealth and power. Those that we used to think were dead tell us that wealth and power are the toughest machines to master in this spiritual gym, and the easiest ways to set ourselves back spiritually. As Jesus says, **"How hard it is for those who are wealthy to enter the kingdom of God!"** (LK 18:24) **"No one can serve two masters; for either he will hate the one and love the other, or he will be devoted to one and despise the other. You cannot serve God and wealth"** (MT 6:24). **"Do not store up for yourselves treasures on earth, where moth and rust destroy, and where thieves break in and steal. But store up for yourselves treasures in heaven, where neither moth nor rust destroys, and where thieves do not break in or steal; for where your treasure is, there your heart will be also** (MT 6:19-21). As He reminds us when He uses the analogy of the camel going through the eye of the needle, which was an ancient gate so narrow that pack animals had to be unloaded to pass through it: emphatically, you cannot take earthly wealth with you. And accumulating any more earthly wealth than you need for your body to survive is a distraction from accumulating spiritual wealth, which of course is the only wealth that matters.

Complete Forgiveness is the Key to Rapid Spiritual Growth

Jesus shares with us a fundamental truth. The whole key to spiritual growth is learning to forgive completely. We cannot even begin to love in the way that Jesus insists we must love until forgiveness is our automatic habit. He also tells us what that looks like.

"But I say to you, do not resist an evil person; but whoever slaps you on your right cheek, turn the other to him also. If anyone wants to sue you and take your shirt, let him have your coat also. Whoever forces you to go one mile, go with him two" (MT 5:39-41). It is important to point out here that He *does not* say,

"Grit your teeth and turn the other cheek." No, it is clear that He expects us to act with joy and with a heart full of perfect love for even those who want to do us harm! He says, **"But love your enemies, and do good, and lend, expecting nothing in return; and your reward will be great, and you will be sons of the Most High; for He Himself is kind to ungrateful and evil men. Be merciful, just as your Father is merciful"** (LK 6:35-36).

Jesus makes it clear that our standard of perfection is not the judgmental and imperfect Christian God, but rather it is the genuine God that He tells us is powerful and loving Spirit. **"You have heard that it was said, 'You shall love your neighbor and hate your enemy.' But I say to you, love your enemies and pray for those who persecute you, so that you may be sons of your Father who is in heaven; for He causes His sun to rise on the evil and the good, and sends rain on the righteous and the unrighteous. For if you love those who love you, what reward do you have? Do not even the tax collectors do the same? If you greet only your brothers, what more are you doing than others? Do not even the Gentiles do the same? Therefore you are to be perfect, as your heavenly Father is perfect"** (MT 5:43-48).

So we are meant to forgive everything, no matter what, as if it never had happened at all!

And we are meant to forgive even those who wrong us repeatedly. "Then Peter came and said to Him, "Lord, how often shall my brother sin against me and I forgive him? Up to seven times?" Jesus said to him, **"I do not say to you, up to seven times, but up to seventy times seven"** (MT 18:21-22). The number seven was used in Jesus's time to mean "really a whole lot." What He is telling us here is that forgiveness cannot be just an occasional act, but it must be a constant, inviolate *attitude.*

Christianity Makes it Harder For Us to Learn to Forgive

Nearly everyone finds the complete forgiveness that Jesus expects of us to be a standard impossible to achieve. And after my years of trying to live the Gospel teachings myself, I am coming to see both why those reared as Christians keep tripping themselves up on forgiveness, and how we can make forgiveness work in the way that Jesus means it to work. We can indeed achieve the Lord's forgiveness standard! *But sadly, Christianity as it is now being practiced makes learning to forgive even harder for us.*

Christians face three particular obstacles in their efforts to achieve perfect forgiveness, all of which we can address. And later in this chapter I will share a trick that can help you defeat them all. But first, here are those Christian obstacles:

- **Christians are taught to think of God as judgmental.** We are taught that God is cranky enough to refuse to forgive us for our human failings unless God receives the blood-sacrifice of God's own Son! And when we believe in a God like that, it is easy to let ourselves be unforgiving. We cannot be expected to be even more forgiving than God is, can we?

- **Christians think perfect forgiveness comes only after perfect love.** Most Christians assume that better loving comes first, but in fact the opposite is true. It is learning perfect forgiveness that makes perfecting our ability to love perfectly even possible.

- **Christians in particular find forcing themselves to forgive injuries after they have already happened to be extremely difficult.** Their problem may be the fact that the notion of judgment is so central to Christian theology. But for whatever reason, strictly practicing Christians tend to be an especially judgmental bunch.

I think of forgiving wrongs after they have happened as "bespoke forgiveness," and it flat-out does not work. Bespoke forgiveness requires us to suffer an injury, feel the pain and resentment of it, then wrestle down all the negative feelings it has raised in us so we can grit our teeth and forgive the wrongdoer. It is nearly impossible to do this in a way that is anything more than token, since just saying the words "I forgive you" doesn't heal the wrong. What works much better is what we might call "prevenient forgiveness," where you teach your mind not to resent injuries. So you never again will have anything to forgive!

Learning to Practice Prevenient Forgiveness

I don't know where this exercise comes from. Given how amazingly well it works, I realize it must have come from Jesus; but whether I learned it in kindergarten or whether the Lord whispered it in my ear is something that doesn't matter now. It works. And what is more, I have begun to understand why it works.

We come into our earth-lives with active access to what is estimated to be about thirty percent of our vast, eternal minds, very much as we would strip down to shorts and a T-shirt as we head to the gym. Scientists call what we leave behind in the eternal reality that is our true home our "subconscious mind," but it is in fact our *superconscious* mind. The part that we leave behind seems to make most of the physical decisions, which frees the parts of our minds that we use actively while we are in bodies to concentrate on the only thing that matters about our lives on earth: these earth-minds are designed for rapid spiritual learning. *And they have three specific traits that vastly enhance our ability to grow spiritually.* These limited earth-minds are:

- **Lazy.** They don't hum along like a computer, but rather they casually flow like water. They find the easiest course and take it.
- **Readily adaptable.** If we rearrange whatever used to be their easiest course, our minds will take the new route without hesitation.
- **Governed by habits.** If our minds were not largely habitual in their actions, we would have to spend our days repeatedly thinking through how best to open a door or start a car, or even compose a sentence.

So our earth-minds learn from our daily emotional reactions to our life-events the things that really are important. And they learn from us, too, how they should react to these important events; but they also are happy to disregard whatever we later teach them is *not* important. *And the entire reason why you or I would ever need to forgive anything is the fact that we have inadvertently taught our minds that some things are major threats that we must fight with fear-based rage.*

Whether it is people who annoy us, morning traffic, the stock market, or what the President just said, for most of us a normal day is one continuous round of irritations. But it need not be that way. Becoming angry about things that you cannot change is a destructive adherence to negativity, and a foolish barrier to your spiritual growth. The sooner you are rid of it, the happier you are going to be. Imagine going through days and weeks of time during which irritations both great and small never bother you. Imagine hearing yet another gripe about the office bully, and feeling only compassion for her; imagine watching an evening of TV news, and never being bothered by anything said. ***You can do it! All you need to do is to reprogram your mind. You were the one who taught it to react with anger, and you are the one who easily can teach it never to be angry again.***

If you are zealous about it, this whole process can be largely completed in a month. After that, you will need to be vigilant for perhaps another several months; but fortunately, your mind will be so vastly relieved not to have to keep reacting negatively that this process is amazingly self-reinforcing. I speak about it at more length in *The Fun of Growing Forever*, but I will give you here the bones of this amazing exercise.

When you decide to begin, try to give yourself a few weeks of clean runway. If you have annoying relatives, choose a non-holiday time; or if you suffer work irritations but now is not the time to change jobs, then at least try to use a work vacation to get yourself started. ***Then spend at least three months being alert and never lowering your guard.*** Unless you will give this effort fully three months of continuous vigilance, it still might work to some extent, but it cannot work extremely well. I don't know if this exercise has a name, but I call it just "forgiveness balls."

Whenever you notice something that you suspect will irritate you, use your hands and big sweeps of your arms right away to gather it all up and tamp it down into a nice, tight ball. You can do this in your mind of course, especially if it happens while driving; but it works best if you will ignore how foolish this makes you feel, and simply do it. Use your whole arms to gather every bit of whatever is about to upset you, and make a show for yourself of forming that ball carefully with your hands. Be sure to include any people who might be involved, especially including yourself.

Squash it all down tight. Then push that ball away with both hands as you say aloud, **"I love you, I bless you, I forgive, and I release."**

I never dreamed this would work so well! I began to do it as a short-cut way to manage all the bespoke forgivenesses that were taking up my days. At first, the process of gathering and pushing away might have taken a couple of tries before I had vanquished all my irritations; but I stuck with it, because within a week or two, doing it just once was enough. And I noticed that my irritations were becoming less frequent. I started to think things were getting better.

Then about six weeks into my new forgiveness practice, I noticed that something had just occurred that used to drive me up the wall. I cannot recall now what it was, but I think another driver had cut me off. I used to be a lethally combative driver, but then one day someone did something stupid, and I realized that my need to brake for him was not bothering me at all.

In fact, now nothing was bothering me! Things that used to upset me still were happening, and I noticed them, but now I felt only peace in their presence. I told a friend at the time that almost in a moment I had become internally quiet, still interacting with the world but at a safe remove from it. Somehow all those levers on the outside of me that people and events used to pull so easily and make me crazy had been disconnected on the inside. Now people could pull on them all day long! I still felt no emotion but mildness and peace.

When you have gone in what seems to be only a moment from being someone with a hair-trigger temper to being someone who knows only peace, that is very big news indeed. I started this exercise with no expectations, so it took me awhile to comprehend the extent to which I had been internally changed.

And this change seems to be permanent. For the past ten years I have felt no significant irritations, no anger, no outrage, no negative emotion beyond a sigh or two when something has gone badly wrong. And no fear! At first I thought my new lack of fear was a product of my having finally vanquished humanity's core fear, which is the fear of death. But my lack of fear seems now to be more the product of this internal softness and peace. The Apostle Paul talks about God's **"peace that passes all understanding"** (Phil 4:7) which fills our hearts and minds. It is only now that I know how that feels. How simple this turns out to be!

Learning Perfect Forgiveness is Our Route to Learning Perfect Love

Learning to forgive as Jesus wants us to forgive feels at first like the toughest spiritual lesson there is. But if we stop trying to forgive things *after* they have happened, and instead we re-program our minds to forgive everything that will happen in our future lives, learning to forgive turns out to be easy! And as Jesus says, learning to forgive perfectly is the gateway to everything good. He says, **"Do not judge, and you will not be judged; and do not condemn, and you will not be condemned; pardon, and you will be pardoned. Give, and it will be given to you. They will pour into your lap a good measure—pressed down, shaken together, and running over. For by your standard of measure it will be measured to you in return"** (LK 6:37-38).

Perhaps above all, learning to forgive as Jesus taught us that we must forgive turns out to be the wondrous gateway to the only power there is. Only when we have learned prevenient forgiveness can we even begin to understand how to love. And Jesus told us that love is crucially important. *The core of His Gospel teaching is that we must love God and love one another, and beyond that there is nothing that matters.*

"One of the scribes came and heard them arguing, and recognizing that Jesus had answered them well, asked Him, 'What commandment is the foremost of all?' Jesus answered, **'The foremost is, 'Hear, O Israel! The Lord our God is one Lord; and you shall love the Lord your God with all your heart, and with all your soul, and with all your mind, and with all your strength.' The second is this, 'You shall love your neighbor as yourself'"** (MK 12:28-31). He said, **"You have heard that it was said, 'You shall love your neighbor and hate your enemy.' But I say to you, love your enemies and pray for those who persecute you… For if you love those who love you, what reward do you have? Do not even the tax collectors do the same?"** (MT 5:43-46)

What follows is the most radical call to love without conditions and without limits and no matter what anyone does to you that human beings ever have received! Please read these words slowly, thinking about their meaning and relating that meaning to your own life.

"But I say to you who hear, love your enemies, do good to those who hate you, bless those who curse you, pray for those who mistreat you. Whoever hits you on the cheek, offer him the other also; and whoever takes away your coat, do not withhold your shirt from him either. Give to everyone who asks of you, and whoever takes away what is yours, do not demand it back. Treat others the same way you want them to treat you. If you love those who love you, what credit is that to you? For even sinners love those who love them. If you do good to those who do good to you, what credit is that to you? For even sinners do

the same. If you lend to those from whom you expect to receive, what credit is that to you? Even sinners lend to sinners in order to receive back the same amount. But love your enemies, and do good, and lend, expecting nothing in return; and your reward will be great, and you will be sons of the Most High; for He Himself is kind to ungrateful and evil men. Be merciful, just as your Father is merciful" (LK 6:27-36).

If these words don't hit you as a clout to the head, then you are not really paying attention. If you are honest, you will have to say that you will try your best, but the kind of radical love the Lord insists upon here is beyond what most of us can do. *And this is why He places such a focus on radical forgiveness first of all.* I used to think He was trying to prepare us for our post-death need to forgive ourselves, but that is small potatoes compared to this need to become sufficiently spiritually advanced that we can readily love and bless our greatest enemies. We cannot love at this level unless we will first learn radical prevenient forgiveness. *And the wonderful thing is that once we have learned to forgive as Jesus wants us to forgive, then loving in the way that He wants us to love turns out to be remarkably easy!*

CHAPTER NINE
WHAT JESUS MEANS WHEN HE TALKS ABOUT LOVE

"I sought my soul, But my soul I could not see. I sought my God, But my God eluded me. I sought my brother, And I found all three."
– William Blake,
English poet, painter, and printmaker (1757-1827)

"Only a life lived for others is a life worthwhile."
– Albert Einstein, German-born
winner of the 1921 Nobel Prize in Physics (1879-1955)

"We might be wise to follow the insight of the enraptured heart rather than the more cautious reasoning of the theological mind."
– A.W. Tozer, American Christian preacher,
author, and magazine editor (1897-1963)

"God loves each of us as if there were only one of us."
– Saint Augustine of Hippo,
North African Christian theologian (354-430)

"We have enough religion to make us hate, but not enough to make us love one another."
– Jonathan Swift,
Anglo-Irish satirist, poet, and cleric (1667-1745)

"Each one of them is Jesus in disguise."
– Saint Teresa of Calcutta, Albanian-Indian Catholic
nun and missionary (1910-1997)

"The doctrines of Jesus are simple and tend all to the happiness of man, that there is only one God and God is perfect. That God and man are one. That to love God with all your heart, and your neighbor as yourself, is the sum of religion. These are the great points on which I endeavor to reform and live my life."
– Thomas Jefferson, 3rd president of the United States
(1743-1826)

*M*astering perfect forgiveness is the key to achieving perfect love. The kind of love that Jesus talks about seems to be impossible for us even to envision until we first have mastered perfect forgiveness; and this is something I could not have understood until I made the Gospel teachings my journey. Make no mistake: achieving the ability to love perfectly is the purpose of your life on earth! Jesus tells us this in various ways, and He even comes right out and says it. **"You have heard that it was said, 'You love your neighbor and hate your enemy.' But I say to you, love your enemies and pray for those who persecute you, so that you may be sons of your Father who is in heaven; for He causes His sun to rise on the evil and the good, and sends rain on the righteous and the unrighteous. For if you love those who love you, what reward do you have? Do not even the tax collectors do the same? If you greet only your brothers, what more are you doing than others? Do not even the Gentiles do the same? Therefore you are to be perfect, as your heavenly Father is perfect"** (MT 5:43-48). So Jesus has given us our task and our challenge. We are to love everyone on earth precisely as everyone is loved by God.

When achieving perfect love is the abiding theme of all four Gospels, and when Christians claim that Jesus is the reason for the religion, it is amazing to see how little effort to teach and practice love at this level is made by any Christian denomination. By my count, the word "love" appears in each of the Books of Matthew and Luke at least a dozen times, in Mark four times, and in the Book of John – the most mystical Gospel – an astounding thirty-eight times. Jesus tells us that perfect universal Love is God's most important law. He says, **"'You shall love the Lord your God with all your heart, and with all your soul, and with all your mind.'**

This is the great and foremost commandment. The second is like it, 'You shall love your neighbor as yourself.' On these two commandments depend the whole Law and the Prophets" (MT 22:37-40).

Modern-Day Christianity Ignores the Importance of Perfect Love

I don't know what more Jesus can do to convince us of love's central importance! But I have been both an ardent protestant and a zealous Catholic, I majored in Christian history in college, and I believed I was going to be a minister. And still, I cannot remember ever being told by any religious figure that love is so important. Both denominations presented love as something more like an icing, a colorful trim, a way to further improve my life rather than something more essential to it.

And as you think about it, that makes human sense. The way we think of love and use the word, it is just a grace-note on our lives. We fall in love; we have children to love; we love our parents and our friends; we even love our pets: but none of this affects who we are. No form of human love is able to change us by one inch! In fact, love as we commonly use the word is largely a feature of the human body. Falling in love is needed for pair-bonding; loving our children is essential to successful reproduction; loving our parents and our friends is how we build the communities that make our survival more likely; and loving our dogs and cats helps to ground us in the inter-species cooperation that until recently was essential to our procuring and preserving a food supply.

But human body-related love like this is ephemeral! Your darling cheated on you? Cross him or her off your list. Your teenager is acting up? Might be time for some tough-love. Your parents don't understand you? Go somewhere else for Thanksgiving. Your friend is telling stories behind your back? Then you have a brand-new enemy! Jesus repeatedly disparages this kind of self-based love, and *A Course in Miracles* refers to it derisively as "special loves." The *Course* tells us that special loves are as counterproductive to our spiritual development as are special hates. Body-based forms of love are all ephemeral and conditional. They continue to shift throughout our lives. *And nothing about these kinds of love has anything to do with the teachings of Jesus.*

The love that Jesus talks about is so different from our usual understanding of love that ideally we would give it a different name. Early Greek translations of the Bible called the lesser forms of body-based love "eros," and they used the word "agape" for the unconditional love that mirrors the perfect love of God. To the modern ear, "agape" sounds like watered-down love, but in fact agape is immensely powerful. *The love that Jesus commands of us is the only love that matters, and at its highest level it is by far the greatest power there is.*

Better Understanding Perfect Love

As we said in Chapter Two, the only thing that objectively exists is what you and I experience as consciousness. Consciousness is in fact a form of energy, and like all forms of energy, it vibrates. We experience its range of vibration as emotions, from fear and anger at the lowest level to perfect love at the highest level, so human emotion is not the ephemeral nothing we long have assumed that it is. Instead, what we experience as emotion is the engine that activates consciousness. *At its higher levels, it is the only power.*

In what we call the afterlife – which is in fact our eternal life – actually raising our spiritual vibration toward ever more perfect love is difficult. We are surrounded by love; we live and breathe love, so in our eternal home we have nothing to push against. But we want to grow spiritually! You and I cannot appreciate while we are in bodies the utter joy that ever more perfect love can bring; but when we are back at home, we crave spiritual growth like every earthly craving put together. It is the only joy, the only power, the only wealth there is. As Jesus says, **"Do not store up for yourselves treasures on earth, where moth and rust destroy, and where thieves break in and steal. But store up for yourselves treasures in heaven, where neither moth nor rust destroys, and where thieves do not break in or steal; for where your treasure is, there your heart will be also"** (MT 6:19-21). Jesus said to a wealthy young man whose spiritual understanding had impressed Him, **"One thing you lack: go and sell all you possess and give to the poor, and you will have treasure in heaven; and come, follow Me"** (MK 10:21). He is saying the same thing to us today.

What Jesus is exhorting us to do is to raise our personal consciousness vibrations away from fear, rage, and the other ishy emotions and toward ever more perfect love. He tells us that as we do this, the kingdom of God will dawn in each of us; and when enough of us have sufficiently raised our personal spiritual vibrations, the kingdom of God will dawn over all the earth.

Achieving the Perfect Love that Jesus Teaches

Here we are nearing the limit of my understanding. As I say in *The Fun of Growing Forever,* my personal efforts to live the Gospel teachings of Jesus as strictly as He means us to live them have produced an extraordinary transformation in me that in retrospect seems to have taken just months, and even after years it seems to be not only permanent but self-reinforcing. *And the Gospel teachings are so ideally suited to modern Western life!* They don't require that we learn to meditate, practice yoga, chant, follow a guru, go to church, or even adhere to any religious rules at all. Those teachings ask of us nothing but a few months during which we will apply them strictly in specific ways, and thereafter they only require that we remain vigilant and ready to reinforce those teachings. *This is so easy! And it is amazingly effective.*

Mastering the process of growing spiritually is going to be essential for everyone who wants to make the most of this earth-lifetime. And since the Gospel teachings are so effective, but apparently almost no one has tried them, we are going to be learning as we go along. But for now, here is what my own experience and the experiences of a few others who have tried the same process suggest is true:

- **Forgiveness is the Key to Learning to Love Perfectly.** If you will rigorously follow the Gospel teachings on forgiveness by learning prevenient forgiveness, you will find that as you shed the dead weight of resentments, petty hates, and petty loves, your spiritual level will begin to rise naturally.

- **Establishing a Gratitude Practice Can be Helpful.** Jesus doesn't talk much about gratitude in the Gospel words that have been preserved, but of course what we have is just a few of the many things that Jesus said to His followers over the more than three years of His ministry. My hunch is that He talked about gratitude in words that to His listeners sounded less radical, and therefore they were less memorable. But developing "an attitude of gratitude" seems to soften our hearts and make both forgiveness and perfect universal love even easier to learn and to practice.

- **You May Need to Minimize Your Ego.** The ego is that petty little fearful and selfish nuisance that keeps tripping you up! It is just a self-preservation feature that – like special loves – is meant to ensure that you will keep your body alive for long enough to learn your spiritual lessons. *It is not who you are.* And as your spiritual vibration begins to rise, your ego may begin to see your spiritual growth as the threat to its survival that in fact it is, so then your ego will find whatever is your own deepest fear and obsess you with it. Years before I began to follow the Gospel teachings, I had used *A Course in Miracles* to smack down my own ego, so as I used the Gospel teachings to raise my spiritual vibration, I didn't have the kind of trouble from my ego that yours might give to you. But I urge you to take the possible advent of any peculiar fears as you are learning perfect forgiveness to be just temporary, and to be a good sign; simply redouble your regular spiritual practice.

- **Vibrating at a Higher Rate Will Naturally Intensify Your Ability to Love.** The effect was so sudden and so transformational that at first I felt as if I was losing some of my love for the people closest to me. But what really was happening was that I was loving other people – even strangers – as I never had before, while at the same time my love for friends and family was becoming less about me and more about them. This is still brand-new for me, this loving all people, and especially this loving those closest to me in a way that does not focus on my own needs, but focuses entirely on theirs. But it is wonderful. Peaceful. Joyous! It feels like love the way love always was supposed to be, and it frees my friends and family from what I can see now was a certain neediness inherent in my special loves. Now I no longer need the adoration of friends and family in order to feel complete in myself. And now I really do love everyone!

So at last we begin to understand what it was that Jesus came to earth to achieve in us. We understand, too, that unless we can empower the Lord to teach the world as He came two thousand years ago to teach the world, humankind faces a future that may be even bleaker than our benighted past. *Jesus is calling to you and me to help Him share the perfect truth of God! The question is: how on earth can we do that?*

CHAPTER TEN
NOT A RELIGION, BUT A WAY OF LIFE

"A small body of determined spirits fired by an unquenchable faith in their mission can alter the course of history."

– Mahatma Gandhi,
Indian spiritual activist (1869-1948)

"Some people don't want to hear the truth because they don't want their illusions destroyed."

– Friedric Nietzsche,
German philosopher (1844–1900)

"Just as a candle cannot burn without fire, men cannot live without a spiritual life."

– Gautama Buddha, Nepalese-Indian sage,
(563 BCE/480 BCE- c.483 BCE/400 BCE)

"You think that your laws correct evil – they only increase it. There is but one way to end evil – by rendering good for evil to all men without distinction."

– Leo Tolstoy, Russian writer (1828-1910)

"Truth is by nature self-evident. As soon as you remove the cobwebs of ignorance that surround it, it shines clear."

– Mahatma Gandhi,
.   Indian spiritual activist (1869-1948)

"If we find the answer to that (why the universe exists), it would be the ultimate triumph of human reason. For then we would know the mind of God."

– Stephen Hawking, English theoretical physicist
and cosmologist (1942-2018)

"The Christian ideal has not been tried and found wanting—it has been found difficult and left untried."

– G. K. Chesterton, English writer, poet, philosopher, and
lay theologian (1874-1936)

"The genuine and simple religion of Jesus will one day be restored: such as it was preached and practiced by Himself."

– Thomas Jefferson,
3rd president of the United States (1743-1826)

*S*implly by reading His Gospel words without reference to the rest of the Bible or to the religion that bears His name, we can see the genuine mission of Jesus.* The fact that the infant religion that became Christianity largely ignored what Jesus had said, and for two thousand years it made Jesus the subject of theories that turn out to be all human-made, may be hard for us to understand. Why did God allow us to get the work of Jesus so wrong for so long? But our perplexity about why the Lord has not until now stepped in to set His work aright doesn't change His Gospel words at all, and nor does it change the almost magical way in which they all fit together. It is essential that we understand what Jesus actually came to do, and the desperate need that He now is proclaiming that we take up His work and help Him to fulfill it.

Jesus came to abolish religions and teach us to relate to God on our own so we can then teach all the world how to love perfectly and forgive completely and thereby bring the kingdom of God on earth. That was the Lord's mission, and it remains His mission. So those of us who are alive today and genuinely want to follow Jesus have before us the incomparable joy of helping Him at last to complete His work, and thereby elevate all of humankind! Let us look at that bolded statement more closely.

Jesus Came to Abolish Religions

Religions are a holdover from the millennia when people served multiple fear-based gods. But then at last the first-century Jews began to see that there is just one God, so Jesus then came as God on earth to help them move past any need for religions. He began by throwing away the entire Old Testament – what the Jews of His day called The Law and The Prophets – and replacing every religious law with God's law of love.

When asked what is the greatest commandment, He said, **"'You shall love the Lord your God with all your heart, and with all your soul, and with all your mind.' This is the great and foremost commandment. The second is like it, 'You shall love your neighbor as yourself.' On these two commandments depend the whole Law and the Prophets"** (MT 22:37-40). He assured us that this abandonment now of all religious laws was a part of God's deliberate plan for humanity when He said, **"Do not think that I came to abolish the Law or the Prophets; I did not come to abolish but to fulfill"** (MT 5:17). And now that they are fulfilled, we won't need the Law or the Prophets any longer.

Jesus spoke out against religious practices frequently, and He especially reviled clergymen. He said, **"Why do you transgress the commandment of God for the sake of your tradition?... You hypocrites! Rightly did Isaiah prophesy of you: 'This people honors me with their lips, but their hearts are far away from me. But in vain do they worship me, teaching as doctrines the precepts of men'"** (MT 15:3-9). And, **"Woe to you, scribes and Pharisees, hypocrites, because you shut off the kingdom of heaven from people; for you do not enter in yourselves, nor do you allow those who are entering to go in"** (MT 23:13). To those who were beginning to build a Jewish sect around Him during His lifetime, He said, **"But no one puts a patch of unshrunk cloth on an old garment; for the patch pulls away from the garment, and a worse tear results. Nor do people put new wine into old wineskins; otherwise the wineskins burst, and the wine pours out and the wineskins are ruined; but they put new wine into fresh wineskins, and both are preserved"** (MT 9:16-17). **"Therefore every scribe who has become a disciple of the** kingdom of heaven is like a head of a household, who brings out of his treasure things new and old" (MT 13:52).

To modern Christians He still is saying, **"Why do you call me 'Lord, Lord,' and do not do what I say?"** (LK 6:46). And, **"Not everyone who says to me, 'Lord, Lord,' will enter the kingdom of heaven, but only he who does the will of my Father who is in heaven will enter"** (MT 7:21). And yet again, right between the eyes: **"If you hold to my teaching, you are really my disciples. Then you will know the truth, and the truth will set you free"** (JN 8:31-32).

Jesus Came to Teach Us How to Relate to God on Our Own

He said, **"Beware of practicing your righteousness before men to be noticed by them; otherwise you have no reward with your Father who is in heaven. So when you give to the poor, do not sound a trumpet before you, as the hypocrites do in the synagogues and in the streets, so that they may be honored by men. Truly I say to you, they have their reward in full. But when you give to the poor, do not let your left hand know what your right hand is doing, so that your giving will be in secret; and your Father who sees what is done in secret will reward you.**

"When you pray, you are not to be like the hypocrites; for they love to stand and pray in the synagogues and on the street corners so that they may be seen by men. Truly I say to you, they have their reward in full. But you, when you pray, go into your inner room, close your door and pray to your Father who is in secret, and your Father who sees what is done in secret will reward you" (MT 6:1-6).

I can add nothing! Jesus's call to leave religions behind and begin to relate to God on our own has been in Christian Bibles for two thousand years.

Jesus Came to Teach the World to Love Perfectly and Forgive Completely

He said, **"You have heard that it was said, 'You shall love your neighbor and hate your enemy.' But I say to you, love your enemies and pray for those who persecute you, so that you may be sons of your Father who is in heaven; for He causes His sun to rise on the evil and the good, and sends rain on the righteous and the unrighteous. For if you love those who love you, what reward do you have? Do not even the tax collectors do the same? If you greet only your brothers, what more are you doing than others? Do not even the Gentiles do the same? Therefore you are to be perfect, as your heavenly Father is perfect"** (MT 5:43-48). And, **"I say to you, do not resist an evil person; but whoever slaps you on your right cheek, turn the other to him also. If anyone wants to sue you and take your shirt, let him have your coat also. Whoever forces you to go one mile, go with him two"** (MT 5:39-41). And,

"Love your enemies, and do good, and lend, expecting nothing in return; and your reward will be great, and you will be sons of the Most High; for He Himself is kind to ungrateful and evil men. Be merciful, just as your Father is merciful" (LK 6:35-36).

When Peter asked him, **"Lord, how often shall my brother sin against me and I forgive him? Up to seven times?"** Jesus said to him, **"I do not say to you, up to seven times, but up to seventy times seven"** (MT 18:21-23).

Jesus is giving us a literal command from God to love perfectly and forgive completely. He even tells us how to do these things, and His lessons work amazingly well. My book, *The Fun of Growing Forever*, demonstrates how we might put the Lord's words into action as we live our lives.

He Came to Bring the Kingdom of God on Earth

How can the most zealous scholars of the most studied words in history have missed the central fact that Jesus came not to start a religion, but instead to make religions obsolete by bringing the kingdom of God on earth?

As Jesus was just beginning to teach, "He came to Nazareth, where He had been brought up; and as was His custom, He entered the synagogue on the Sabbath, and stood up to read. And the book of the prophet Isaiah was handed to Him. And He opened the book and found the place where it was written, **'The Spirit of the Lord is upon Me, because He anointed me to preach the Gospel to the poor. He has sent Me to proclaim release to the captives, and recovery of sight to the blind, to set free those who are oppressed, to proclaim the favorable year of the Lord.'** And He closed the book, gave it back to the attendant and sat down; and the eyes of all in the synagogue were fixed on Him. And He said to them, **"Today this Scripture has been fulfilled in your hearing"** (LK 4:15-21). Then, "after John (the Baptist) had been taken into custody, Jesus came into Galilee, preaching the gospel of God, and saying, **'The time is fulfilled, and the kingdom of God is at hand; repent (**or **"reform your mind") and believe in the gospel'"** (MK 1:14-15). "Soon afterwards, He began going around from one city and village to another, proclaiming and preaching the kingdom of God" (LK 8:1). Jesus talked incessantly about the kingdom of God and His role in bringing about the advent of the kingdom of God. For example, He once told His listeners, **"I must preach the kingdom of God to the other cities also, for I was sent for this purpose"** (LK 4:43). He said, **"The Law and the Prophets were proclaimed until John** (the Baptist)**; since that time the gospel of the kingdom of God has been preached, and everyone is forcing his way into it** (LK 16:16). (Perhaps His crowds were growing?) And He said, **"How shall we picture the kingdom of God, or by what parable shall we present it? It is like a mustard seed, which, when sown upon the soil, though it is smaller than all the seeds that are upon the soil, yet when it is sown, it grows up and becomes larger than all the garden plants and forms large branches; so that the birds of the air can nest under its shade"** (MK 4:30-32). **"The kingdom of God is not coming with signs to be observed; nor will they say, 'Look, here it is!' or, 'There it is!' For behold, the kingdom of God is in your midst"** (or "is within you") (LK 17:19-21).

Jesus sent His disciples out to spread His Gospel teachings as a new spiritual movement and thereby help to bring the kingdom of God on earth, not just to preach a Jewish sect that was based in human ideas. He said, **"All authority has been given to Me in heaven and on earth. Go therefore and make disciples of all the nations... teaching them to observe all that I commanded you; and lo, I am with you always, even to the end of the age"** (MT 25:18-20).

How Can We Help the Lord Complete His Mission?

Until recently I had assumed that we who seek to follow the teachings of Jesus would never be able to call ourselves Christians. Surely that name would make people think we must believe the whole range of Christian dogmas? But I am coming now to see that we are Christians in the only meaningful sense of the word, since we are doing the Lord's announced work from its beginning, where it remains primary and untarnished. We are sitting at His feet two thousand years ago and finding truth and love and a solid path forward for despairing humankind in these teachings that have come to us as the gift of a perfectly loving God.

Just imagine the joy of hearing those earliest teachings from the Lord's own lips! The promised Messiah is in our midst, and He is sharing with us a new understanding of God as loving Father, and not as cranky and judgmental despot. Read the Gospel words on forgiveness, love, and the advent of the kingdom of God on earth, and imagine the wonder of being the first to hear those words as Jesus spoke them. Imagine breaking bread with Him and sharing the thrill of His daily walk, never knowing what He might say next. And then imagine Him telling us that the gift of teaching these essential truths brought to us directly from the only God is going to be our own! He is giving us His Great Commission, little altered after two thousand years for the different times in which we live. He says:

"Behold, I send you out as sheep in the midst of wolves; so be shrewd as serpents and innocent as doves. But beware of men, for they will hand you over to the courts … and you will even be brought before governors and kings for My sake … But when they hand you over, do not worry about how or what you are to say; for it will be given you in that hour what you are to say. For it is not you who speak, but it is the Spirit of your Father who speaks in you" (MT 10:16-20).

"Therefore do not fear them, for there is nothing concealed that will not be revealed, or hidden that will not be known. What

I tell you in the darkness, speak in the light; and what you hear whispered in your ear, proclaim upon the housetops…. Are not two sparrows sold for a cent? And yet not one of them will fall to the ground apart from your Father. But the very hairs of your head are all numbered. So do not fear; you are more valuable than many sparrows" (MT 10:26-31).

I think now that indeed we must call ourselves Christians! And as Jesus the Christ uses you and me to begin at last His movement to uplift in Spirit all of humankind, we might rehabilitate what for the past two thousand years always should have been a title not of fear and faith and pointless dogmas, but only of joy in the certainty of God's perfect love.

Our Need to Avoid Religiosity

The greatest tragedy to befall our efforts would be for them to devolve into just one more religion! Religions are systems by which a few use fear-based dogmas to control us while they interpose themselves between God and all the people they are supposed to serve. *And every religion is a fly in amber.* It might still preserve the appearance of truth, but that truth has been killed by the pretty amber of human culture and traditions, so it is immutable now. Profoundly dead. If we never forget that this work is the Lord's and nothing about it belongs to us, then perhaps we will be able to avoid assuming the leaden chains of religiosity. But we must never forget this greatest of all risks!

Instead, we must be like Jesus's first disciples. They called this new movement to spread His genuine Gospel teachings "the Way," perhaps because He had said, **"My teachings are the way, and the truth, and the life; no one comes to the Father but through my teachings"** (JN 14:6). To us He says freshly what He said to them: **"You are the salt of the earth; but if the salt has become tasteless, how can it be made salty again? It is no longer good for anything, except to be thrown out and trampled under foot by men. You are the light of the world. A city set on a hill cannot be hidden; nor does anyone light a lamp and put it under a basket, but on the lampstand, and it gives light to all who are in the house. Let your light shine before men in such a way that they may see your good works, and glorify your Father who is in heaven"** (MT 5:13-16).

We must not forget that our job is to shine the Lord's light into every corner of the world! We are just the candles. The Lord is the light.

The Lord's Directives

Jesus told us what the parameters of our work must be, and He emphasized three points in particular:

- **We must be servants.** Our discovery of the genuine Jesus and our feeling called now to share His Gospel words could be giving us heads the size of Manhattan. Jesus contended with this problem among His earliest followers, who soon came to think that they were hot stuff, too. "They came to Capernaum; and when He was in the house, He began to question them, **'What were you discussing on the way?'** But they kept silent, for on the way they had discussed with one another which of them was the greatest. Sitting down, He called the twelve and said to them, **'If anyone wants to be first, he shall be last of all and servant of all'** (MK 9:33-35). "And He said to them, **'The kings of the Gentiles lord it over them... But it is not this way** with you, but the one who is the greatest among you must become like the youngest, and the leader like the servant. For who is greater, the one who reclines at the table or the one who serves? Is it not the one who reclines at the table? But I am among you as the one who serves'" (LK 22:25-27). "The disciples... said, 'Who then is greatest in the kingdom of heaven?' And He called a child to Himself and set him before them, and said, **'Truly I say to you, unless you are converted and become like children, you will not enter the kingdom of heaven. Whoever then humbles himself as this child, he is the greatest in the kingdom of heaven. And whoever receives one such child in My name receives Me'"** (MT 18:1-5).

- **We must not fight old-style Christianity.** We can see the religion shriveling around us, and seeing the great harm it continues to do in preventing broader awareness of the Gospel truths might tempt us to believe that it is one of our tasks to kill it off altogether. *But that is not what Jesus wants us to do!* To us, the prevailing versions of Christianity must be as the prevailing versions of Judaism were to the Lord when He walked the earth. He used them as examples of specious spirituality, and He urged us not to be like their clergy. But far from attempting to destroy Judaism, He suggested that His listeners take His teachings and simply follow them separately. He said, **"But no one puts a patch of unshrunk cloth on an old garment; for the patch pulls away from the garment, and a worse tear results. Nor do people put new wine into old wineskins; otherwise the wineskins burst,** and the wine pours out and the wineskins are ruined; but they put new wine into fresh wineskins, and both are preserved" (MT 9:16-17). He urged clergymen to teach both their old religion and His new Gospels at the same time, but separately. He said, **"Therefore every scribe who has become a disciple of the kingdom of heaven is like a head of a household, who brings out of his treasure things new and old"** (MT 13:52). When His disciples complained to Jesus that someone other than His core followers was casting out demons in His name, Jesus said, **"Do not hinder him; for he who is not against you is for you"** (LK 9:50). For Jesus, all that mattered was bringing as many people as possible to a better understanding of His Gospel truths. He didn't want Judaism to dilute His pure message, but neither did He want people to feel forced to choose to follow either the old way or the new. It will be so important that we who serve the Lord will devoutly adhere to His example! Ultimately, we know that God's truth will prevail.

- **We must not have expectations.** Personally, I find these Gospel revelations to be so perfect and so uplifting that I expect them to transform the world by Tuesday. But we are not in charge. We are, as Jesus repeatedly reminds us, servants. And He assures us that if we will sow sufficient seeds, there will be a bountiful harvest. He says, **"Behold, the sower went out to sow; and as he sowed, some seeds fell beside the road, and the birds came and ate them up. Others fell on the rocky places, where they did not have much soil; and immediately they sprang up, because they had no depth of soil. But when the sun had risen,**

they were scorched; and because they had no root,
they withered away. Others fell among the thorns,
and the thorns came up and choked them out. And
others fell on the good soil and yielded a crop, some
a hundredfold, some sixty, and some thirty" (MT 13:3-
8).

Jesus sent His followers to walk from village to village. In His
day there was no more rapid way to reach and educate people. At
first, He urged them to keep to Jewish villages, perhaps because
His teachings had been tailored to be best understood by the
world's first true monotheists. But when members of the Samaritan
minority proved to be even more receptive, the Gospel teachings
were preached in their villages as well.

*Our great good fortune is the fact that in the Internet age, we
can reach everyone!*

Some of what Jesus says suggests that even back when He was
still on earth, He was foreseeing a much better day when
humankind will have moved beyond religions and toward
developing for each of us our individual relationships with God.
Here is a lesser-known example from His conversation with the
Samaritan woman at the well. The Samaritans' worship was
centered on their holy mountain, Mount Gerizim, while the Jews'
holy Temple was in Jerusalem.

"The woman said to Him, 'Sir, I perceive that You are a
prophet. Our fathers worshiped in this mountain, and you people
say that in Jerusalem is the place where men ought to worship.'
Jesus said to her, **'Woman, believe Me, an hour is coming when
neither in this mountain nor in Jerusalem will you worship the
Father. You worship what you do not know; we worship what
we know.... But an hour is coming, and now is, when the true
worshipers will worship the Father in spirit and truth.... God is**

spirit, and those who worship Him must worship in spirit and truth'" (John 4:19-24).

We will be learning as we go along how best to share these Gospel truths, and early experimentation will be important. We might find not one best way, but many! We must not fight traditional Christianity, but we will want to get the Lord's truth out and make it commonly known, because as traditional Christianity withers and dies, it must not be allowed to take Jesus with it. Eventually it may be essential that He be more forcefully separated from that old-time religion, but that will never be our decision, and it never will be our task. Every decision must be the Lord's. We are servants, and we are useful to Jesus only if we keep our servants' heart. This is such an exciting time to be alive! *Historical hindsight may eventually suggest that our now being able to confirm the truth of the genuine Gospel teachings of Jesus was a literal miracle that occurred at almost the final moment in history before the negativity that is now rampant on earth tipped all of humanity into fear-based chaos.*

Jesus calls to us now as He called to Peter and Andrew when He first began His work. "Now as Jesus was walking by the Sea of Galilee, He saw two brothers, Simon who was called Peter, and Andrew his brother, casting a net into the sea; for they were fishermen. And He said to them, **'Follow Me, and I will make you fishers of men.'** Immediately they left their nets and followed Him" (MT 4:18-20).

You and I are being given the same invitation that Jesus extended to His earthly disciples. After two thousand years, humankind at last can learn and live these eternal truths! As Moses said almost 3500 years ago, **"the eternal God is a dwelling place, and underneath are the everlasting arms"** (Deut 33:27).

Appendices

APPENDIX I
BRIEF SUGGESTED STUDY GUIDE

*Y*ou may find this book hard to believe until after you have done some of your own research. Fortunately, afterlife-related evidence is abundant now and widely available; and if you want some personal pointers, the books suggested here are some of my favorites. Everyone who has an obsessive hobby is unable to believe that others don't share it, but you may already have your own hobbies. If you want to cut to the chase, I will first give you eight central resources. Read only these, and then go back to living your life with the glorious understanding that those who have gone ahead are fine, they always are only a thought away, and meanwhile the greatest gift you ever can give to them, and give to yourself, is your own further spiritual growth. Or if you find that you have more time, Appendix II is a more extensive guide where I can welcome you into sharing my passion.

Eight Key Resources

The first book given here summarizes the quantum physics that governs our greater reality in a way that non-scientists can enjoy. The second is an accurate afterlife account that was recently written by an elevated being who teaches the newly-dead how to communicate with those left behind. The third is the venerable classic in this field. And the fourth is reportedly an analysis of the Gospels by the One who truly knows them best. All are brief and easy to understand and a lot of fun to read, so please read them first. And the four books that follow them are the absolutely stunning work of one of the world's leading experts on the greater reality and what actually is going on. If you have the time, please read these eight books, and then go on with my love to enjoy your best and most joyous possible life and afterlife!

- *Quantum Enigma* (2006) - Bruce Rosenblum and Fred Kuttner have so much fun with the physics of consciousness that they have done what I would have thought would be impossible. They have written an enjoyable physics page-turner.

- *Flying High in Spirit - A Young Snowboarder's Account of His Ride Through Heaven* (2015, 2018) – Mikey Morgan, with the help of his mother, Carol, has written an extraordinary and easily understood summary of his own afterlife experiences. Mikey is a very high-level being, reportedly now upper sixth level, who had last lived on earth in the 1600s. He wanted to be able to communicate with you and me in modern terms, so he took a twenty-year additional earth-lifetime that ended in 2007. Now he communicates through his mother by pendulum, and he teaches people who are newly arrived in the afterlife how to send their families signs of their survival. Everything he tells us is amply corroborated by other communicators. For someone so spiritually advanced to be communicating with us in the 21st century as a modern American kid makes his book important, and it is a cheerful delight to read!

- *Matthew, Mark, Luke, and John* - The red letters in any modern translation of these four slim books of the Christian Bible are the only place where the words of

Jesus are preserved. Early church councils edited the Gospels, both removing things that Jesus had said and adding bits about church-building, sheep-and-goats, and Apocalyptic warnings that Jesus could not have uttered; but otherwise, the words of Jesus in the Gospels are amply corroborated by what the dead now tell us. Appendix III of The Fun of Dying, The Fun of Staying in Touch, and The Fun of Growing Forever will give you further details about the correspondences between the genuine teachings of Jesus and the modern afterlife evidence.

- *Liberating Jesus* (2015, 2021) - Roberta Grimes received this book during two weeks of time from an entity who reportedly was Jesus. Many of those who have fallen away from strict Christian practice love *Liberating Jesus*; although for devout Christians, what it has to say about the religion can be troubling to read.

Dr. R. Craig Hogan is among the world's leading experts on the greater reality. He has lately produced four books that together provide a college-level course on the afterlife and what actually is going on. These books are so terrific that they ought to be on everyone's reading list!

- *Your Eternal Self: Science Discovers the Afterlife* (2021) - This is the updated and expanded second edition of Dr. Hogan's 2008 breakthrough treatise about what actually is going on. Your mind is not produced by or contained in your brain. And your mind is an individual expression of the Universal Intelligence of which we all are a part —we really are all one Mind!

- *Reasons for What Happens to You in Your Life and Your Afterlife: Revealed by Speakers in the Afterlife* (2021) - Dr. Hogan uses information from residents of the life after this life to help to explain what happens to each of us through all the major stages of life: deciding to enter Earth School; planning the Earth School experience; learning to succeed in Earth School; growing in love, compassion, and understanding; graduating; and living in the life after the Earth School life.

- *There Is Nothing but Mind and Experiences* (2021) - Here Dr. Hogan explains that the Universal Intelligence is the basis of reality, and we are all individual expressions of it. He explains how we know this is true, and what it means for your life.

- *Answers to Life's Enduring Questions: Given by Science Discoveries and Afterlife Revelations* (2021) - This is an easy-to-read summary of the contents of the other three books. It is meant primarily for people who want the information but not the detailed explanations and evidence.

These eight works will give you some of the best current information about what makes eternal life possible, what the afterlife is like, how our loved ones communicate with us, and how to make the most of this lifetime so you can have your best eternal life. Perhaps that will be enough. If it is, just let me add that if you ever have questions, you can contact me at *www.RobertaGrimes.com* and I will do what I can to find your answers.

Appendix II
REFERENCES LIST

You may be able to perfectly and joyously inhabit the eternal life that is your birthright only after you have done some of your own research. To aid you in that process, here are more than seventy books on seventeen primary topics that I have found to be useful as we work to better understand what actually is going on.

I. Things Are Not What They Seem

Given the depth and range of the afterlife-related evidence now available, it is a sorry fact that the mainstream scientific community continues to ignore it, and even tries to debunk it. This scientific stonewalling is millennia old, although its more active phase seems to have begun at the start of the twentieth century, just as the pioneering quantum physicists were proving that things are not what they seem. Fortunately, dedicated folks have been studying the evidence on their own, so this lack of curiosity on the part of mainstream scientists is little more than an inconvenience.

- *A Lawyer Presents the Evidence for the Afterlife* (2013) - Victor Zammit and Wendy Zammit have spent decades gathering and presenting afterlife evidence to anyone who will listen. If you are having trouble accepting the fact that there even is an afterlife, here is where you might begin your education.

- *Your Eternal Self: Science Discovers the Afterlife* (2021) - R. Craig Hogan gives us an updated and expanded second edition of his 2008 breakthrough treatise about what actually is going on. Your mind is not produced by or contained in your brain. And your mind is an individual expression of the Universal Intelligence of which we all are a part —we really are all one Mind!

- *Reasons for What Happens to You in Your Life and Your Afterlife: Revealed by Speakers in the Afterlife* (2021) - R. Craig Hogan uses information from residents of the life after this life to help to explain what happens to each of us through the major stages of life: deciding to enter Earth School; planning the Earth School experience; learning to succeed in Earth School; growing in love, compassion, and understanding; graduating; and living in the life after the Earth School life.

- *There Is Nothing but Mind and Experiences* (2021) - R. Craig Hogan here explains that the Universal Intelligence is the basis of reality, and we are all individual expressions of it. He explains how we know that this is true, and what it means for your life on earth.

- *Answers to Life's Enduring Questions: From Science Discoveries and Afterlife Revelations* (2021) - R. Craig Hogan here gives us an easy-to-read summary of the contents of his other three books that were issued in 2021. This fourth volume is meant primarily for people who want the perspectives but not the detailed explanations and evidence.

- *The Biology of Belief* (2005) - Bruce Lipton is a cell biologist who got off the mainstream science reservation and never looked back. Like Hogan's books, Lipton's is so fundamental that it should be one of the first things you read as you get your feet wet in doing wider research. Lipton also recorded a CD set called The Wisdom of Your Cells that makes a great companion to his book.

- *Is There Life After Death?* - Elisabeth Kubler-Ross was a physician who specialized in death and dying, and this CD story of her personal journey – told in her wonderfully-accented voice – is compelling. If you don't make the time to listen to Kubler-Ross, your life will forever be the poorer for it.

- *The Secret Life of Plants* (1972) - Half a century ago, Peter Tompkins and Christopher Bird wrote such an extraordinary book that I am amazed that so few people have heard of it. It is a long book, and not directly on point, but if you have the time, please read it. I read this book when it was first published, and even today I wince a little when I cut a tomato or grate a carrot.

II. Consciousness as the Source of Reality

The conclusion that consciousness is the source of reality will come to you only gradually, as you read more and more death-related evidence and you realize there is no other explanation. If you want to speed up the process, here are ten very different books, four of them by physicists, which should get you there more quickly.

- *Quantum Enigma* (2006) – Bruce Rosenblum and Fred Kuttner are adventurous academic physicists, and here they give us an enjoyable summary of their understanding of the consciousness issue in quantum physics. This book is plainly written and highly accessible for non-physicists, so it gives you a great place to begin your physics studies.

- *The Idea of the World (2019); Why Materialism is Baloney* (2014) – Bernardo Kastrup is a brilliant young Dutch scientist who has written a half-dozen scholarly but very accessible books that point to the non-material nature of reality. Here are the two that are most relevant to our research.

- *The Self-Aware Universe* (1995) – Amit Goswami is a physicist who understands many of the implications of quantum theory. His book is a little tough for non-physicists. And because it takes into account only Eastern religious teachings, it can be a struggle for the rest of us to grasp. Still, it is fascinating support for the fundamental truth that Consciousness (or Mind) is all there is.

- *The Physics of Consciousness* (2000) – Evan Harris Walker was another physicist. He is said to have been the founder of the modern science of consciousness research, and although he tries to simplify the physics, his book can be a tough slog in spots. Still, I loved every mind-bending minute of it. Walker died in August of 2006. After more than fifty years apart, he is again with Merilyn, the love of his life, who died when they were both sixteen, and (his dedication says) "without whom there would be nothing."

- *My Big TOE* (2007) – Thomas Campbell is a physicist whose consciousness theory of everything is entirely consistent with what afterlife researchers have learned independently. I first met Dr. Campbell soon after this book was published, and I was astounded to see how close his theory of everything based in traditional physics was to the one that I had developed using the afterlife evidence. What wonderful validation! His book is meant for physicists, so it is another hard slog for laypeople. But it is altogether worth the effort.

- *The Unobstructed Universe* (1940) – Stewart Edward White worked in the 1930s. You will be astonished to find that more than seventy-five years ago he was writing about consciousness as the source of reality, the indestructibility of consciousness, and so much else! There are few books so basic. You will enjoy both him and his psychic/spirit wife, although you may find this book (if at all) only in an antique paperback.

- *Our Unseen Guest* (1920) – Darby and Joan (pseudonyms) worked with Stephen (also a pseudonym), a soldier killed in World War I, and a century ago they published a seminal account which identifies consciousness as the source of reality. The first half of their book is an insightful study of the problems inherent in communicating through mediums. The second half is the earliest reasonably accurate account of the reality revealed by the afterlife evidence that I have yet found. I feel about this book very much as I felt when I realized how completely modern evidence agrees with the teachings of Jesus in the Gospels: if they got it right so long ago, then Darby and Joan both reinforce and are reinforced by what the evidence now tells us. And when eventually some physicist is acclaimed as the mother of a consciousness theory of everything, she ought at least to acknowledge the fact that plucky young Stephen was there long before.

- *The Conscious Universe* (1997); *Entangled Minds* (2006) – Dean Radin is an academic parapsychologist whose interest lies in the workings of psychic phenomena in a quantum reality. Dubbed by some "the Einstein of consciousness research," he never quite says that everything springs from consciousness. But his books are filled with evidence of the primary role of consciousness, and they are well done and fascinating reading.

III. The Nature of Your Mind

If you have trouble grasping the fact that your brain does not generate your mind, here are some books to help you better understand what and where your mind is, and also how powerful it is. Like it or not, the reality you create is your own!

- *Brain Wars* (2012) - Mario Beauregard is a professor of neurology and radiology who has written an engrossing and highly readable summary of the battle now raging between scientists who are still trying to find a source of the human mind inside the brain, and those who have come to accept the fact that the human mind is separate and pre-existing. If you are having trouble making this important leap of understanding, then Beauregard's book is for you.

- *An End to Upside-Down Thinking – Dispelling the Myth That the Brain Produces Consciousness, and the Implications for Everyday Life* (2018) - Mark Gober has written a smart and highly enjoyable summary of the modern case against scientists' erroneous assumption that the brain generates consciousness.

- *The Holographic Universe* (1991) - Michael Talbot's masterwork remains a classic in this field. Much more evidence has been developed in the decades since this author published and soon thereafter died young, but his book remains one of the most important resources on this subject.

- *The Field* (2001) - Lynne McTaggart is an essential pioneer in this area. This book is indispensable background, and she also recorded two wonderful CD sets called *The Field* and *Living the Field* if you would rather listen than read.

- *The Power of Eight - Harnessing the Miraculous Energies of a Small Group to Heal Others, Your Life, and the World* (2017) - Lynne McTaggart's more recent book is a wonderful guide to using the power of our minds in practical ways to improve our lives.

- *One Mind: How Our Individual Consciousness is Part of a Greater Consciousness and Why it Matters* (2014) - Larry Dossey, MD is a scientist who follows the lead of physicists Max Planck and Albert Einstein in explaining what underlies reality in simple terms that laypeople can understand. For you to begin to internalize the true nature of your mind and the nature of God will considerably aid your efforts to grow spiritually.

- *The Divine Matrix* (2007) - Gregg Braden is another pioneer in helping us to understand where and what our minds really are, and his book is fascinating and highly readable.

IV. The Post-Death Realities

We have nearly two hundred years of abundant and consistent communications from the dead, most of the best of which were received in the late nineteenth and early twentieth centuries. The fact that there are so many communications, and they have been coming to us for so long, from different parts of the world and in a number of different ways, is not what is most significant. *What still astounds me is the fact that all these hundreds of communications describe the same complex and wonderful post-death reality!* In decades of reading afterlife communications, I have never found an outlier. I will here give you some of what afterlife experts consider to be the best summaries, together with two older channeled works that are believed by experts to be genuine.

- *Flying High in Spirit – A Young Snowboarder's Account of His Ride Through Heaven* (2015, 2018) – Mikey Morgan with the help of his mother, Carol, has written an extraordinary and easily understood summary of his own afterlife experiences. Mikey is a very high-level being, reportedly now upper sixth level, who had last lived on earth in the 1600s. He wanted to be able to communicate with you and me in modern terms, so he took a twenty-year additional earth-lifetime that ended in 2007. Now he communicates through his mother by pendulum. Everything he tells us is amply corroborated by other communicators. For someone so spiritually advanced to be communicating with us in the 21st century as a modern American kid makes his book important, and it is a cheerful delight to read!

- *The Afterlife Revealed – What Happens After We Die* (2011) – Michael Tymn is a venerable expert in the field of afterlife communication, and his brief book is a wonderfully detailed summary of what we learn from studying afterlife communications.

- *The Afterlife Unveiled* (2011) – Stafford Betty is a professor of religion, and a good friend of Michael Tymn's. Their books – both brief and easy to understand – make great companion volumes for people beginning to understand the afterlife realities.

- *The Fun of Dying – Find Out What Really Happens Next!* (2010, 2015, 2021) – Roberta Grimes wrote a brief explanation of the afterlife realities for laypeople. This book is meant specifically for those who need an easy summary of this information because they themselves are sick or because a loved one has just died, but general readers have called it an easy and happy way to begin their afterlife studies.

- *Afterlife Interrupted – Helping Stuck Souls Cross Over* (2018) – Nathan Castle is a Dominican priest who helps people who died in an accident, in battle, or otherwise at a time other than at a planned exit point, and who then were in the grasp of such severe negative emotions that they did not completely transition. Fr. Nathan helps them to complete their journeys home. The process he describes is perfectly consistent with what we know about the afterlife and the greater reality, and this wonderful book breaks some amazing new ground!

- *Life in the World Unseen* (1954) – Robert Hugh Benson was a Catholic priest who discovered after he transitioned that his book, *The Necromancers* (1907), was altogether wrong. So through his friend, Anthony Borgia, he wrote a series of books, of which this is the first and the best. In fact, many researchers consider this to be the most comprehensive and accessible account of the afterlife ever communicated to us. I urge everyone who has any interest in this field to read it, especially since it is now available for free on the Internet.

- *Testimony of Light* (2009) – Frances Banks was an Anglican nun who died in 1965, and whose account of the period soon after her death is full of beautiful and touching stories and gorgeous scenes, all consistent with the rest of the evidence.

V. The Design and Functioning of Other Realities

Our biggest problem in studying the realities that we enter at death is that we must get our information from fallible human beings. Whether they speak from beyond the veil, or, like Bob Monroe, they only visited the extra-material realities and returned, our reporters often know little more than we know, believe it or not. This means that it is important to read many after-death accounts, since the more of them we read, the more we can see that each is giving us a slightly different miniscule glimpse of what is the same gigantic set of after-death realities.

- *The Place We Call Home – Exploring the Soul's Existence After Death* (2000) – Robert J. Grant gives a brief and lucid examination of the extra-material realities based primarily on the Edgar Cayce materials. I have concerns about relying on Cayce because some of his predictions have been wrong. (Actually, my studies suggest legitimate reasons for his errors, but a treatise on Cayce is, like so much else, beyond the scope of this book.) Because Grant's book is simply written, and what he reports is reasonably consistent with other sources, his book may be a good introduction.

- *Journeys Out of the Body* (1971); *Far Journeys* (1985); *Ultimate Journey* (1994) – Robert Monroe was a successful businessman with an interesting hobby. At about age 40, he learned how to leave his physical body whenever he liked and travel in extra-material realities, which afterlife researchers call the astral plane. A bright and ruthlessly honest researcher, he wrote three books that together present a gripping story of his own development. Monroe's books detail these realities from the viewpoint of someone who has not died, and therefore he was not protected in his travels as you and I will be at death. From his out-of-body perspective we see less of the scenery and more of the scaffolding. What is interesting about his books to me is the fact that nevertheless Monroe describes essentially the same beyond-material realities that we discover from other sources. His perspective lets us better appreciate how lovingly the post-death process is designed to protect and nurture our minds.

- *Cosmic Journeys* (1999) – Rosalind A. McKnight was one of Bob Monroe's Explorers, the volunteers who replicated his out-of-body work under laboratory conditions. Her book describes her experiences as a naïve and untrained but fearless participant. The first part is a bit silly, but the second half is great, and the view of astral reality that she sets forth here is amply corroborated elsewhere.

- *After We Die, What Then? (1987); Enjoy Your Own Funeral* (1999) – George W. Meek spent his retirement studying the after-death realities. His books are easy and enjoyable reads, and they contain useful diagrams of the upper levels and the nesting of your various bodies – so long as you always remember that all the levels and bodies exist in the same place (to the extent that talking about "place" means anything). Meek was an important Instrumental Transcommunication (ITC) and Electronic Voice Phenomena (EVP) pioneer, so his books also contain interesting sections on these topics.

- *Journey of Souls* (1994); *Destiny of Souls* (2000) – Michael Newton hypnotically regressed a number of people in deep trance to what they said were their lives between lives, and he reported in these books what they told him. After having read many tales from dead people, I was astonished to read these books and find that the accounts they contained were different from most of the others. They seemed oddly impersonal, even mechanical, although the after-death process that they described was consistent with what I had found elsewhere. It was only later that I thought about the possibility that when we are under deep hypnosis, we may be accessing our eternal subconscious (or superconscious) minds rather than the conscious minds of the individuals who have just died. If that is true, then these books are interesting for that fact alone. Most of what they say is reasonably consistent with other evidence, although they also contain some things that I have not been able to corroborate. These shouldn't be the first books on this topic that you read, but later on if you are curious and open-minded, you might enjoy them.

- *Our Unseen Guest* (1920); *The Unobstructed Universe* (1940) – Darby and Joan and Stewart Edward White were colleagues a century ago, and the two books listed here are the earliest reasonably accurate modern summaries of afterlife details that I have found. The fact that I came across them only after I had pieced together most of this from other sources made them astounding to me, although if I had read them decades ago, I might not have taken them seriously. These books are highly readable, and you will find them to be both informative and still on the cutting edge. I urge you to read them, even though you will find them only in libraries or in used paperbacks.

VI. Near-Death Experiences

We are consistently told by those who are dead that death is always a one-way trip, and people who return from NDEs never actually reach the afterlife levels. This is why many accounts of their experiences are aberrant and tinged with religious symbols meant to comfort them. The primary value to the rest of us of stories told by NDE experiencers is the wonderful sense that most of them have of an all-pervading love, and the plain assurance that people's minds can function independently of their bodies. Since they are coming back, those assisting experiencers through their NDEs and back into their bodies will give them only experiences that will further their earthly spiritual growth, and will work to avoid burdening them with imagery that might confuse or trouble them.

- *Evidence of the Afterlife* (2010) - Jeffrey Long, with Paul Perry, has published what is billed as the largest study of near-death experiences ever conducted. It focuses on statistical compilations of many experiences gleaned through his website, and it also shows how common NDE details (like the fact that those blind from birth are able to see during NDEs) help to prove the reality that our minds can function apart from our bodies. Long and Perry claim that their book "reveals proof of life after death." If you need to see such proof before you venture ahead, then their book is for you.

- *Beyond the Light* (Revised Edition – 2009) - P.M.H. Atwater had three NDEs in 1977, and she spent the next four decades investigating the phenomenon. NDEs are highly variable from individual to individual, but they are consistent across cultures. The fact that infants and young children have the same experiences that adults do (except that they don't have unpleasant NDEs) helps to prove that NDEs are more than just suggestion-induced fantasies. Atwater has written more than a dozen good books, including the enormous and daunting **The Big Book of Near-Death Experiences** (2007), but this one seems to be the best for our purposes.

- *Life After Life* (1975); **The Light Beyond** (1988) - Raymond A. Moody, Jr., is the first popularizer of near-death experiences, and by now he is something of a legend. The experiences that he describes are commonly reported by people who attend a lot of deaths.

- **Ordered to Return** (originally published as **My Life After Dying**, 1991) - George G. Richie, Jr., had what may be the most elaborately detailed near-death experience ever, and his brief book is a classic in this field. Moody calls it "the best such book in print."

VII. Deathbed Visions

Less well known today than near-death experiences are deathbed visions, even though they appear to be a universal part of dying. All the books listed here are enjoyable and fascinating, and I suggest that you read at least one of them.

- **Death-Bed Visions** (1926) - Sir William Barrett wrote what remains the classic work on deathbed visions, and his brief book is a wonderful read. Unfortunately, it is long out of print and it may be hard to find. Reading it made me see how sad it is that today most dying people are so well sedated that they (and we) miss some wonderful experiences during the moments that they spend in two realities.

- *At the Hour of Death* (1977) - Karlis Osis and Erlendur Haraldsson detail a study of some 50,000 terminally ill patients observed just before their deaths by a thousand doctors and nurses in the United States and in India. Osis and Haraldsson are able to rule out medical explanations for these patients' before-death visions, and they show us that these experiences are much the same in both cultures.

- *One Last Hug Before I Go* (2000) - Carla Wills-Brandon's summary of modern deathbed visions and other before-death and at-death phenomena is a worthy successor to Sir William's pioneering volume. It was this book that helped me understand why it is that deathbed visions may be necessary. Those newly freed from their bodies are apparently so clueless and confused that without the guidance of dead loved ones and guides they can easily go off-track.

- *Glimpses of Eternity* (2010) - Raymond A. Moody, Jr. has done it again! Having coined the term "Near-Death Experience," he went on thirty-five years later to coin the term "Shared Deathbed Experience." His research indicates that some of those sitting at the bedsides of the dying will see the visions of loved ones and the next levels of reality that the dying typically see, and some even leave their bodies and join the departing spirit on the first part of its journey. As is true of everything that Raymond Moody and Paul Perry write together, this book is an easy and enjoyable read.

- *In the Light of Death* (2015) - Ineke Koedam is a Dutch researcher whose important book is a powerful contribution to the literature of deathbed experiences.
- *Words at the Threshold* (2017) - Lisa Smartt conducted a broad study of the things that dying people say in the days and weeks before they transition, and the result is a fascinating compilation which includes some phenomena that have not previously been observed.

VIII. Signs and Messages from the Dead

Those living on the afterlife levels are far more aware of us than we are of them, and naturally our grief pains them very much. It seems that millennia ago, dead people learned how to manipulate our reality with their minds so they could send us signs of their survival. By now, it seems to be an almost universal phenomenon that those who transition successfully will pause to send a few comforting post-death signs before they venture forth to enjoy the glorious afterlife realities.

- *Hello from Heaven!* (1995) - Bill Guggenheim and Judy Guggenheim wrote a voluminous book on spontaneous signs received from the dead. Often the closest survivors of those who are recently dead will experience communications of various kinds, and some of them are spectacular! Indeed, it has been estimated that more than half of widows and widowers see a vision of the departed spouse within the first year. The Guggenheims interviewed some 2,000 people and collected and categorized more than 3,300 accounts of their experiences.

- *Messages* (2011) - Bonnie McEneaney lost her husband in the World Trade Center Towers on 9/11. Soon thereafter, she began to receive signs from him, and other survivors heard from their lost loved ones as well. McEneaney collected many of these accounts into a book that also includes premonitions and messages received in other ways. This is a beautiful and moving account of a group of people who left their homes one morning not expecting that they were about to die, and then they were desperate to assure their families that they were still okay.

- *Afterlife Communication* (2014) - Expert presenters at the 38th Annual Conference of The Academy f or Spiritual and Consciousness Studies assemble chapters on the current state of play concerning sixteen proven methods of afterlife communication and eighty-five accounts of extraordinary communications facilitated by these methods. Despite the bounty of information this book contains, it is an easy and enjoyable read.

- *The Fun of Staying in Touch* (2014, 2016, 2021) - Roberta Grimes presents a simple summary of the types of signs that the dead typically send to us, and also of some of the methods of communication that we can initiate with them.

- *The Survival of the Soul and its Evolution After Death* (1921, 2017) - Pierre Emile Cornillier was a meticulous researcher whose wonderful book containing an amazing three hundred and seventy-odd pages of séances held during the heyday of physical and deep-trance mediumship has recently been republished.

IX. Spiritual and Psychic Mediums

I still have trouble believing in the work of mental mediums. I can't get past the fact that they are mind-reading with dead people! And often the dead people whose minds mediums are reading are their own guides, which guides are in contact with our dead relatives. It all feels too tenuous to me. But that is just me. Gary Schwartz's book has convinced me that my prejudices are wrong, and I have recently come to understand that good spiritual and psychic mediums can be very good indeed.

- *The Afterlife Experiments* (2002) - Gary E. Schwartz of the University of Arizona is one of very few academically trained scientists who are investigating the afterlife evidence in a traditional university setting. Something of a skeptic himself, he uses strict scientific methods to study psychic mediums under laboratory conditions with remarkable success. For this book, he subjected some of the most prominent living mediums to double-blind and triple-blind experiments, and he found in some cases that the odds against chance for the results of their readings were in the multiple millions to one.

- *The Amazing Afterlife of Animals: Messages and Signs from Our Pets on the Other Side* (2017) - Karen A. Anderson has made a specialty of assisting bereaved pet owners by receiving for them messages from their recently departed pets.

X. Physical and Deep-Trance Mediums

The late nineteenth and early twentieth centuries were the heyday of physical and deep-trance mediums. What appears to be needed for talented living psychics to develop these skills is many years of passively sitting in the dark night after night, and in the days before radio there were folks who started with fads like table-tipping and went on to become amazingly good trance mediums. Physical mediums in trance are able to produce extraordinary phenomena and even full materializations, and deep-trance mediums can withdraw from their bodies and let a dead medium (called a control) speak, using the living medium's vocal cords. Recent efforts to resurrect both skills in Great Britain and in the United States are showing some initial promise, but the journey to full development for a talented trance medium is a long one! Meanwhile, I have given you here a recent encyclopedic compendium; two recent books about physical mediumship; two important books by a current leading afterlife researcher; a fascinating set of early accounts by a different researcher; and also three accounts of the work of an important early-twentieth-century team.

- *Great Moments of Modern Mediumship – Volume I* (2014) - Maxine Meilleur has assembled a breathtakingly complete account of the various kinds of afterlife evidence to be found in the annals of mediumship, from the mid-nineteenth century onward.

- *Unfolding Physical Mediumship: Historical, Philosophical, and Personal Perspectives* (2018) - Susan Barnes has written an excellent and easily read summary of the overall history and the current state of play in physical mediumship.

- *In Pursuit of Physical Mediumship* (2007) - Robin Foy has a long personal history in the field of modern British physical mediumship, notably including his involvement in the Scole Experimental Group. His book is a colorful journey though his personal experiences in the field.

- *The Articulate Dead – They Brought the Spirit World Alive* (2008) - Michael Tymn is a venerable expert in the field of afterlife research. This is his seminal book on the heyday of evidential afterlife communication.

- ***Resurrecting Leonora Piper: How Science Discovered the Afterlife*** (2013) - Michael Tymn's book about the "white crow," Leonora Piper, is a must-read.

- *Spectral Evidence I & II* (2017 & 2018) - Riley Heagerty has made a career of researching and bringing to light the more obscure aspects of the heyday of spirit communication around the turn of the 20th century. His books are dead-on accurate, and they read like candy.

- ***Some New Evidence for Human Survival*** (1922); ***Life Beyond Death with Evidence*** (1928); ***In the Dawn Beyond Death*** (late 1930s) - Charles Drayton Thomas was a British Methodist minister who worked with a deep-trance medium named Gladys Osborne Leonard and her dead control, Feda. He was a curious and methodical fellow investigating what he saw as a cutting-edge phenomenon that was delivering world-changing information. Reading these books in order gives you a sad sense of what a lost period the whole twentieth century really was. Scientists had spent the latter part of the nineteenth century disparaging and trying to debunk all evidence related to mental telepathy and other psi phenomena. Then the early twentieth century brought a flood of afterlife communications produced through deep-trance mediums, so scientists of the day changed their tack. They began to insist that these were not communications from the dead at all, but the mediums were reading the minds of living relatives. So then some of the teams of dead collaborators who were working with deep-trance mediums set out to prove their existence to scientists by devising clever tests for themselves which would rule out the possibility of mind-reading. Thomas's 1922 book is less interesting to us than are the other two listed here because most of it is patient documentation of the results of these self-tests by the dead delivered to help scientists overcome their skepticism. The dead passed nearly all their own tests, so by the time of Thomas's 1922 book, mainstream science had changed its course again and was ignoring all phenomena that did not fit with materialism. If you have never heard of Charles Drayton Thomas and his century-old book of proofs that were given by his dead collaborators, you know that even then mainstream science's stonewalling was sadly effective.

XI. Automatic Writing

Some of the most interesting first-person accounts by dead people have been received by means of automatic writing. Someone with mediumistic ability sat with pen in hand or with fingers on the keys, and a dead person with similar abilities then wrote as if those hands were his own. The books listed here are quick and enjoyable reads, and nearly all of what they tell us is amply corroborated elsewhere. If you can accept how they were received, they are a useful introduction to the post-death realities.

- *Life in the World Unseen* (1954); *More About Life in the World Unseen* (1956) – Robert Hugh Benson was a British

Catholic priest who died in 1914 and discovered after his death that some of what he had written during his lifetime about the afterlife was wrong. So through his friend, Anthony Borgia, he wrote these corrective manuscripts. I came across his books late in my research, and I found them to be so consistent with what I had already learned from other sources as to be frankly astonishing. No matter where these two volumes came from, they are useful first-person accounts of how the afterlife levels can appear to those who are newly arrived.

- *The Book of James* (1974) – William James and Susy Smith wrote an entertaining book that is mostly consistent with the rest of the evidence. William James, the brother of novelist Henry James, was a late-nineteenth-century Harvard professor of psychology and the first president of the American Society for Psychical Research. Susy Smith was a psychic and a prominent researcher during the 1970s, when this book was dictated.

- *Testimony of Light* (1969) – Frances Banks and Helen Greaves have given us a fascinating portrayal of Banks's early adjustments to life after death. Banks was an Episcopal nun and a spiritual seeker all her life. So many of the details of her account of what happened to her after her death are so consistent with other evidence that her slim volume is well worth reading.

XII. Guided or Induced Afterlife Connections

The afterlife evidence and insights provided by quantum physics seem more and more to suggest that everything that we consider to be real is happening in what we might begin to think of as a universal Mind of which each of our minds is a part. So it shouldn't be surprising that some of the most promising research into personal contact with the dead involves communications that seem to be happening in our minds, while at the same time they are happening in an external and palpable reality. I cannot explain this promising new field, so I'll let some of its pioneers do that for you.

- *Induced After-Death Communication: A Miraculous Therapy for Grief and Loss* (2014) – Allan L. Botkin, Raymond Moody, and R. Craig Hogan have updated and reissued a remarkable book that Botkin and Hogan first co-authored a decade ago.

- *Guided Afterlife Connections* (2011) – Rochelle Wright and R. Craig Hogan are among the pioneers of an extraordinary set of procedures that enable grieving people to meet with, talk with, laugh with, and even hold hands with and hug their dead loved ones. I have met some of the earliest experiencers and heard directly from them about meetings with the dead that seemed to be almost unbelievable. The proof was in the pudding, though: people who had been distraught with grief told me that their grief had been nearly eliminated altogether in one session. Some of them now enjoy regular visits with a dead husband or child. Amazing.

- *Reunions: Visionary Encounters with Departed Loved Ones* (1994) – Raymond A. Moody, Jr. and Paul Perry describe Moody's extensive work in the 1980s with a psychomanteum patterned on the Oracle of the Dead that was used for 2500 years at Ephyra in ancient Greece. Moody and his clients have had considerable success with this method of contacting the dead. He continues to offer the use of his psychomanteum to seekers, but he tells us that the process of preparation is extensive and "is not to be taken lightly."

XIII. ITC and EVP

Instrumental Transcommunication (ITC) and Electronic Voice Phenomena (EVP) are in their infancy, but this field of research begins to show such promise that we can now pretty well foresee that within a few decades electronic communication with the dead will likely be common. As is true of so much of what is involved in getting this information to the world, the most important ITC and EVP researchers are teams of dead scientists. The biggest barrier to advancement in this area has long been a deficit of living researchers who could act as these dead scientists' patient and very-long-term laboratory assistants. That problem seems to be ending, however, and the dead now working in this field seem to be feeling a new urgency about making breakthroughs.

- *Miracles in the Storm* (2001); *Spirit Faces* (2006) - Mark Macy has for decades been at the center of ITC and EVP research, and his books are a good introduction to these subjects. The first book listed here details how almost a decade of promising research fell apart in the late 1990s because clashes among some of the living researchers caused their dead collaborators to withdraw. The second book includes a summary of some extra-material details gleaned from Borgia's Life in the World Unseen as well as two similar primary sources.
- *Electronic Voices* (2010); *Glimpses of Another World* (2021) - Anabela Cardoso is a venerable Portuguese researcher

working with an eminent team of the dead. She has achieved some extraordinary results.

XIV. Group Contacts

What is needed for real evidential contact to take place between our level of reality and the levels occupied by the dead is the sincere long-term commitment of living people to the process. The dead know who is genuine and who is not, and sometimes when they find a group that seems to them to be worth the effort, a team of the dead will begin what for them is a difficult process and use their living collaborators as a way to deliver validating evidence. The best ITC and EVP have been produced this way, as have been most other remarkable proofs, like apports (items materializing in air), images produced on film, and even human materializations. I have never heard of a team of dead collaborators who began the process and then tired of it, but living people seldom devote the time and energy required for more than a few years' time; and shockingly, sometimes the mischievous dead will interrupt the most successful group experiments. What happened briefly in the village of Scole in Norfolk, England, in the mid-nineties is an example of the sort of wonderful result that can be obtained by dedicated living researchers who are willing to let their dead collaborators take the lead.

- *The Scole Report* (1999) – The most extensive report to date on collaborations with the dead is available as a research paper that was printed in the Proceedings of the Society for Psychical Research, Volume 58, Part 220, in November of 1999. You can find it in many university libraries, and if you resort to copying it you will want to make color copies of its wonderful illustrations. *The Scole Report* describes a scientific investigation of some extraordinary validations that were visited on The Scole Experimental Group from 1993 through 1998 at Scole in Norfolk, England.

- *The Scole Experiment* (1999) – Grant and Jane Solomon worked with the Scole Experimental Group to summarize the findings detailed in *The Scole Report* for general readers. When you read this book, be aware that the full *Scole Report* is even more wonderful.

XV. Reincarnation

There is so much evidence for reincarnation that clearly something like it happens. It's a difficult process to understand, however, since time is not objectively real, so somehow all our lives on earth are happening at the same time. Accounts from upper-level beings suggest that we think of reincarnation not as a linear process, but more as a vat from which the bucket of each lifetime is dipped and back into which each lifetime is poured. Who knows? If you wonder about reincarnation, here are a few good books on the subject.

- *Reliving Past Lives* (1978) – Helen Wambach's groundbreaking study of mass hypnotic regressions is a brief and fascinating book. She set out to disprove reincarnation by hypnotically regressing thousands of people to lives lived in specific historical periods, expecting to be able to record an inconsistent mess of fantasy and gibberish. What she found instead was a distribution of thousands of memories of past lives that included genders, locations, clothing, utensils, foods, and other small details which so perfectly matched the historical record that to have achieved these results by chance was nearly mathematically impossible.

- *Twenty Cases Suggestive of Reincarnation* (1971); *Unlearned Language* (1984); *Where Reincarnation and Biology Intersect* (1997) – Ian Stevenson was Chairman of the Department of Psychiatry at the University of Virginia, and he was a leading researcher in the field of reincarnation. Stevenson spent a half-century studying cases of young children who remembered recent previous lives that had ended violently, and the result is a spectacular body of work which will be celebrated only when the rest of modern science catches up with it. Stevenson wrote for scientists, so his writing style is dry. But the work that he details in his dozen or more volumes is overwhelming evidence for prompt reincarnation in what appears to be the narrow case of unexpected violent death. These are three of his seminal works.

- *Many Lives, Many Masters* (1988); *Same Soul, Many Bodies* (2004) – Brian Weiss is the foremost popularizer of past-life regression therapy for use in the treatment of medical and psychological problems. An eminent Yale-trained psychiatrist, Weiss accidentally discovered the effect that apparent past lives can have on our present life. Unlike other regression therapists who have made the same discovery, he risked his medical career to get the word out. He has even ventured into the newer field of progression therapy (the investigation of how our future lives might affect the present one), which consciousness theory suggests should be possible, although it is a lot harder for us linear-thinking humans to grasp. The result is two illuminating books that offer a good introduction to the whole topic of reincarnation.

- *Children's Past Lives* (1997); *Return from Heaven* (2001) – Carol Bowman has studied the past-life memories of children, and while most of Stevenson's subjects remembered only their most recent lives, Bowman studied children whose present lives appeared to have been affected by traumas suffered in more distant lifetimes. She also has studied the phenomenon of children quickly reincarnating within the same family, which appears to happen fairly often when infants or toddlers die.

- *Reincarnation – The Missing Link in Christianity* (1997) – Elizabeth Clare Prophet wrote a scholarly but highly readable exposition of reincarnation as an original Christian belief. People who doubt that reincarnation was taught and believed by the earliest Christians owe it to themselves to read this book.

- *Your Soul's Plan* (2009) – Robert Schwartz wrote the definitive work on the fact that nearly all of us write life-plans before our births, and these can contain what we might consider to be negative events. Understanding why sometimes very bad things happen for our own spiritual good can help us to make the most of crucial lessons, and might perhaps reduce the need for us to return for additional lifetimes.

XVI. Spirit Influence and Possession

You may or may not take seriously something for which there is considerable evidence: it seems to be possible for living people to be influenced or even possessed by spirits of the dead. Indeed, the condition may even be common, and it may be the cause of any number of otherwise inexplicable maladies. Who knows? Unlike mediumship and near-death experiences, possession has scarcely been studied at all, and spirit-releasement therapy is seldom practiced now because state regulators and malpractice insurers frown on it. This attitude can be expected to change once eternal Mind is shown to be the source of reality. Meanwhile, those few therapists who have made their careers in spirit-releasement therapy (the process of coaxing possessing beings away from their victims and toward the loved ones waiting for them) have had such apparent success that you may find these books fascinating.

- *People Who Don't Know They're Dead* (2005) - Gary Leon Hill wrote a quick and enjoyable book that is a useful introduction to the topic.
- *Healing Lost Souls* (2003) - William J. Baldwin was a late-twentieth-century expert in this field.

XVII. Achieving More Rapid Spiritual Growth

There have been a number of good things to come from the nascent science of afterlife studies, even beyond the obvious boon of our knowing at last that our minds really are eternal. We also have learned from the dead why we even take lifetimes on earth at all: we come here to raise our personal spiritual vibrations away from fear and toward more perfect love, just as Jesus tells us is true in the Gospels. As the truth about reality becomes more widely known, and as our need to achieve rapid spiritual growth becomes foremost in more of the developed world, there will be many new resources to aid us. For now, here are some important books to help you in your quest for spiritual growth.

- *Matthew, Mark, Luke, and John* - The red letters in any modern translation of these four slim books are the only place in the Christian Bible where the words of Jesus are preserved. Early church councils edited the Gospels, both removing things that Jesus had said and adding bits about church-building, sheep-and-goats, and Apocalyptic warnings that Jesus could not have uttered; but otherwise, the words of Jesus in the Gospels are amply corroborated by what the dead now tell us. Appendix III of *The Fun of Dying, The Fun of Staying in Touch*, and *The Fun of Growing Forever* gives you details about the amazing correspondences between the genuine teachings of Jesus and the modern afterlife evidence.

- *Awaken with Gratitude* (2016) - Hillis Pugh is a guru of gratitude. He teaches it, and he can help you understand how to use it to its best effect.

- *Conscious Being* (2015) - TJ Woodward's book rocked my world. Here are the essential Gospel teachings, arrived at from the perspective of Eastern writings! TJ writes beautifully and very accessibly. If you really cannot stand to think of doing anything related to the Bible, then perhaps his book will be enough for you; although once you have begun to work on forgiveness, I hope you will soon realize that you also need to forgive Christianity.

- *A Course in Miracles* (1992, 2008, 2009) - Helen Schucman with the help of William Thetford received between 1965 and 1972 this set of Text, Workbook for Students, and Manual for Teachers that apparently was channeled by a team that Jesus led. Wherever the *Course* came from, it is a powerful set of lessons in ultimate forgiveness. If you are ready to try for Level Six of the afterlife realities at the end of this lifetime, then doing the *Course* may be your best shot! Beware, though. The *Course* is heavy learning, and it is very hard to manage on your own. Fortunately, there are *A Course in Miracles* study groups in most cities worldwide.

- ***Quantum Forgiveness*** (2015) - David Hoffmeister is a student of A Course in Miracles who uses movies as modern-day parables to give us another approach to learning forgiveness.

- ***Liberating Jesus*** (2015, 2021) - Roberta Grimes received this book during two weeks of time from an entity who reportedly was Jesus. Many of those who have fallen away from strict Christian practice love *Liberating Jesus*, although for devout Christians what it has to say about the religion can be troubling to read.

APPENDIX III
PLUCKING BITS OF COAL FROM AMONG THE DIAMONDS

The words of Jesus in the Bible are "as easily distinguishable as diamonds in a dunghill."

– Thomas Jefferson,
3rd president of the United States (1743-1826)

When we were treating the whole Christian Bible as the Inspired Word of God, we were stuck with accepting whatever those Bible words might say. Now we understand, however, that none of the Bible is magically the Inspired Word of God. Now we are able to verify by using nearly two centuries' worth of afterlife evidence that only major parts of the four Gospels can be independently corroborated. We are even able to further refine what within the Gospels themselves Jesus likely did say and what He likely did not say.

Fortunately, most of what Jesus is quoted as saying in the Gospels can be seen to be consistent with the afterlife evidence and with other things that He is reported to have said. But still, there are bits of coal that a careful reader can distinguish and pluck from among what Thomas Jefferson referred to as the diamond words of Jesus. And it is important that we make an effort to discover and remove that coal, since in some cases it very much distorts the actual message of Jesus.

Truth is truth! And only the truth is what Jesus wants to put into our hands. In general, if something Jesus is quoted as saying in the Gospels is (a) inconsistent with other things that Jesus is quoted as saying in the Gospels; (b) inconsistent with the afterlife evidence; and perhaps even (c) just what those who were establishing Roman Christianity would have wanted Jesus to say, then chances are good that we have spotted some coal.

Here are a Few Examples

As you read and reread the Gospel red letters, you will become ever better at distinguishing those passages that simply do not fit with the rest. What has felt beautiful about this process for me is that in trying to sort wheat from chaff in the Gospels, I have had to examine the red letters closely. In doing that, I have come to know Jesus as I never had before. His love, His wisdom, and the astonishing perfection of His teachings shine for me even brighter. *His words in the Gospels are diamonds indeed!*

I should especially note that as we have studied the afterlife evidence, we have come to know the genuine God as perfect, universal love devoid of human failings. So anything that makes God seem to be less than perfect cannot have come from Jesus. In addition, of course, any reference in the Gospels to "thrones," the "elect," the "end times," or "sin" as the breaking of arbitrary rules is derived from Christian theology and therefore must be a later edit.

- It is important to be alert for terms that are anachronistic, erroneous, or doctrinal. In the passage quoted below, we notice the anachronistic reference to a "church," the erroneous reference to a gated Hades, the impossible reference to handing "the keys of the Kingdom of Heaven" to a human being, the notion of "binding" on earth being in any way applicable to God, and of course the fact that this passage is exactly what the church-builders would have wanted Jesus to say. We should note, too, that "Petros" for "rock"

would be a pun in Greek, but Jesus spoke Aramaic. Here is the most blatant later addition of them all:

"I also say to you that you are Peter, and upon this rock I will build My church; and the gates of Hades will not overpower it. I will give you the keys of the kingdom of heaven; and whatever you bind on earth shall have been bound in heaven, and whatever you loose on earth shall have been loosed in heaven" (MT 16:18-19).

This next example is inconsistent with both the afterlife evidence and the meaning and tone of most other Gospel passages. It gives clergymen a handy threat to keep their flocks in line. It inserts the idea of a cross long before Jesus died on one. It warns us that we might lose our soul, when in fact that is impossible. And the last sentence is an anachronistic and erroneous reference to events imagined in the Book of Revelation. This passage is a particularly unpleasant lump of coal that we can gladly toss:

"Then Jesus said to His disciples, **'If anyone wishes to come after Me, he must deny himself, and take up his cross and follow Me. For whoever wishes to save his life will lose it; but whoever loses his life for My sake will find it. For what will it profit a man if he gains the whole world and forfeits his soul? Or what will a man give in exchange for his soul? For the Son of Man is going to come in the glory of His Father with His angels, and will then repay every man according to his deeds'"** (MT 16:24-27).

- Some bits of coal are given away by their references to theological concepts that would have been unknown to Jesus. For example, the whole notion of a Trinity was proposed only after Jesus was crucified. Every Trinitarian reference in the Gospels therefore is a frank anachronism. So we must remove what would otherwise be an important sentence from the Great Commission:

"And Jesus came up and spoke to them, saying, **'All authority has been given to Me in heaven and on earth. Go therefore and make disciples of all the nations,** (~~baptizing them in the name of the Father and the Son and the Holy Spirit~~), **teaching them to observe all that I commanded you; and lo, I am with you always, even to the end of the age'**" (MT 28:18-20).

- Some obvious coal is cultural. When a passage has medieval details and a medieval feel to it, and especially if it doesn't fit particularly well with either the rest of the Gospels or the afterlife evidence, then we have found a later edit. The core of this story – that what we do for the least person we are doing for Jesus – is beautiful, and it is true; but all this talk of a King and a throne and nations gathering must be later cultural edits. The notion that Jesus will return "in His glory" smacks of a fictitious End Times. And of course, the afterlife evidence and the Gospel words of Jesus insist that each of us is perfectly loved, and neither God nor Jesus ever will judge us, so all that nonsense about sheep and goats gets pitched into the dustbin as well:

"But when the Son of Man comes in His glory, and all the angels with Him, then He will sit on His glorious throne. All the nations will be gathered before Him; and He will separate them from one another, as the shepherd separates the sheep from the goats; and He will put the sheep on His right, and the goats on the left. Then the King will say to those on His right, 'Come, you who are blessed of My Father, inherit the kingdom prepared for you from the foundation of the world. For I was hungry, and you gave Me something to eat; I was thirsty, and you gave Me something to drink; I was a stranger, and you invited Me in; naked, and you clothed Me; I was sick, and you visited Me; I was in prison, and you came to Me.'

"Then the righteous will answer Him, 'Lord, when did we see You hungry, and feed You, or thirsty, and give You something to drink? And when did we see You a stranger, and invite You in, or naked, and clothe You? When did we see You sick, or in prison, and come to You?'

"The King will answer and say to them, 'Truly I say to you, to the extent that you did it to one of these brothers of Mine, even the least of them, you did it to Me'" (MT 25: 31-40).

Here below is another parable with a similar message. We know from the afterlife evidence that there is no fiery hell. We also know that eternal damnation cannot happen. But Jesus may indeed have told a story that was something like this, thinking that those who in this lifetime fail to make spiritual progress might after death consign themselves to the outer darkness for a time:

Jesus presented another parable to them, saying, **"The kingdom of heaven may be compared to a man who sowed good seed in his field. But while his men were sleeping, his enemy came and sowed tares among the wheat, and went away. But when the wheat sprouted and bore grain, then the tares became evident also. The slaves of the landowner came and said to him, 'Sir, did you not sow good seed in your field? How then does it have tares?'**

"And he said to them, 'An enemy has done this!'

"The slaves said to him, 'Do you want us, then, to go and gather them up?'

"But he said, 'No; for while you are gathering up the tares, you may uproot the wheat with them. Allow both to grow together until the harvest; and in the time of the harvest I will say to the reapers, 'First gather up the tares and bind them in

bundles to burn them up; but gather the wheat into my barn'" (MT 13:24-30).

What follows is Jesus's reported explanation for this parable. From the thought that Jesus Himself sowed the good seed while an imaginary devil sowed the weeds right through to the notion of end times and a blazing furnace, this whole explanation is a later fabrication. By now, you should be spotting the signs:

"And He said, **'The one who sows the good seed is the Son of Man, and the field is the world; and as for the good seed, these are the sons of the kingdom; and the tares are the sons of the evil one; and the enemy who sowed them is the devil, and the harvest is the end of the age; and the reapers are angels. So just as the tares are gathered up and burned with fire, so shall it be at the end of the age. The Son of Man will send forth His angels, and they will gather out of His kingdom all stumbling blocks, and those who commit lawlessness, and will throw them into the furnace of fire; in that place there will be weeping and gnashing of teeth. Then the righteous will shine forth as the sun in the kingdom of their Father. He who has ears, let him hear'"** (MT 13:37-43).

The whole of Matthew 24 is devoted to end-times prophecy (similar passages are in Mark 13 and in Luke 21:8-36). I have read this chapter repeatedly, trying to figure out what Jesus might have said that could have been the basis for so much that is inconsistent with the teachings of Jesus, and also with the afterlife evidence. All I can conclude is that the Bible-builders wanted to tie the Book of Revelation directly back to Jesus, so they cribbed some of its ideas into His Gospels. When Jesus came to teach us how to use our many earth-lifetimes to better grow toward spiritual perfection, it is beyond nonsensical that He ever would have said, **"This gospel**

of the kingdom shall be preached in the whole world as a
testimony to all the nations, and then the end will come" (MT
24:14). Are we to imagine that Jesus came to teach us how to bring
the kingdom of God on earth, and at the same time He intended to
end the world as soon as everyone had been reached but before the
kingdom of God could be manifest? The only part of this whole
chapter that rings true is the Lord's assurance that **"Heaven and
earth will pass away, but my words will not pass away"** (MT
24:35).

*- And then there are references to an appalling barbarism that
still is at the core of Christian traditions.* There is no evidence that
having taken Christian communion makes any spiritual difference,
whether on earth or in the afterlife levels. If we want to limit our
reading of the Gospels to just what Jesus probably said, then we've
got to turn each description of the Last Supper into a convivial
farewell to friends in which Jesus asks them to remember Him
whenever they dine together. It is impossible now to know
whether the passage that follows is a complete addition, or
whether it is the corruption of something that Jesus said about His
teachings being as essential as food and drink. We may never
know. What we do know is that Jesus never said anything like this!
To this day, He likely remains appalled that you might believe that
He ever said it:

"So Jesus said to them, **'Truly, truly, I say to you, unless you
eat the flesh of the Son of Man and drink His blood, you have no
life in yourselves. He who eats My flesh and drinks My blood
has eternal life, and I will raise him up on the last day. For My
flesh is true food, and My blood is true drink. He who eats My
flesh and drinks My blood abides in Me, and I in him. As the
living Father sent Me, and I live because of the Father, so he who**

eats Me, he also will live because of Me. This is the bread which came down out of heaven; not as the fathers ate and died; he who eats this bread will live forever'" (JN 6:53-58).

- There is a series of important Gospel phrases where Jesus is seen to be using a personal pronoun in a way that is out of character. It seems likely that to first-century people, their shorthand use of "I" or "me" for "my teachings" in reporting the words of Jesus would have seemed harmless. But it is clear to a modern reader, in view of the fact that religious affiliations are irrelevant when it comes to getting into heaven, that in each of these cases what Jesus was really talking about was His teachings:

"I am the way, and the truth, and the life. No one comes to the Father but through me" must actually have been said something like "My teachings are the way, and the truth, and the life. No one comes to the Father but through my teachings" (JN 14:6).

"I am the resurrection and the life; he who believes in Me will live even if he dies, and everyone who lives and believes in Me will never die" surely was said something more like "My teachings are the resurrection and the life. He who believes my teachings will live, even if he dies, and everyone who lives and believes my teachings will never die" (JN 11:25-26). Note here, too, that for Jesus to be referring to His resurrection years before His death is an anachronism that means that we likely should pitch this whole passage as a suspect addition.

"For God so loved the world that He gave His only begotten Son, that whoever believes in Him shall not perish, but have eternal life" has to have been said something more like "For God so loved the world that He gave His only begotten Son, that whoever believes His teachings shall not perish, but have eternal life" (JN 3:16).

Correcting all such mistakes is important, since there is no objective evidence whatsoever for sacrificial redemption, substitutionary atonement, or the notion that only professed Christians will get into heaven.

- Some bits of coal can be spotted by the way they mischaracterize God. The genuine God that both Jesus and the dead describe is infinitely powerful and perfectly loving Spirit, devoid of human failings. The Old Testament God in the minds of those who were constructing the Christian Bible was a vastly expanded human being. You will see it is easy to tell the difference!

"What He has seen and heard, of that He testifies; and no one receives His testimony. He who has received His testimony has set his seal to this, that God is true. For He whom God has sent speaks the words of God; for He gives the Spirit without measure. The Father loves the Son and has given all things into His hand. He who believes in the Son has eternal life; but he who does not obey the Son will not see life, but the wrath of God abides on him" (JN 3:32-36).

God has no wrath! Jesus doesn't "give" the Spirit, but rather each human being is part of God as Spirit. The teachings of Jesus are not rules to be obeyed, but rather they are a prescription for living our best eternal lives. The notion of Father, Son, and Spirit is a later Trinitarian reference. And finally, neither God nor Jesus ever is our afterlife judge, as Jesus explicitly tells us. Tossing this one out is an easy call. And it is important that we toss it! On the day when I first wrote these words, I drove past a billboard that depicted a fiery hell and inquired whether passers-by knew where they would be going if they died tonight. That billboard cited John

3:36, the last sentence in the passage above. This sort of triumphal unleashing of an imaginary vengeful God against people Jesus says that we must only love is one of Christianity's most repugnant fruits.

And finally, here is a passage that we can imagine might have been, at its base, something that Jesus could have said. His efforts to wean people away from their religious superstitions began to cause disruptions within families, and as Jesus's time here grew short, you can see in some Gospel passages a little impatience that He hasn't made more progress. He may well have said in exasperation some version of, **"Look, this is going to get a lot harder. Who is with me?"** An exhortation to greater devotion and renewed effort. I don't buy the parts of this that seem ego-related, like **"worthy of me"** and **"for my sake,"** because that simply is not Jesus: His life on earth was an exercise in humility. I don't buy the anachronistic reference to the cross, either. But Jesus could see that His work was disrupting His disciples' personal lives, and He might well have dealt with that problem frankly. Even so, it is nonsensical to do as Christians do so often, and see a passage like this that is reflective of a long-ago moment in time as Jesus prophesying events that were going to happen thousands of years later.

"Do not think that I came to bring peace on the earth; I did not come to bring peace, but a sword. For I came to set a man against his father and a daughter against her mother, and a daughter-in-law against her mother-in-law; and a man's enemies will be the members of his household.

"He who loves father or mother more than Me is not worthy of Me; and he who loves son or daughter more than Me is not worthy of Me. And he who does not take his cross and follow

after Me is not worthy of Me. He who has found his life will lose it, and he who has lost his life for My sake will find it" (MT 10:34-39).

Reading the Gospels Attentively

We understand now that Jesus is a genuine historical figure. His Gospel words can be studied and verified, and the evidence now strongly suggests that He brought to us the easiest method for achieving rapid spiritual growth ever devised. Trying to appreciate ever better what it was that the Lord must actually have said, what He meant by it, and how we can apply His words to creating our best eternal lives as we share His truth with all the world can be our lifelong pleasure! The teachings of Jesus in the Gospels are demonstrated now to be the living Word of our infinitely loving God. And it is only when we follow them with joy as the philosophy that they are meant to be that we can at last begin to make our best eternal spiritual progress.

APPENDIX IV
READING JESUS IN LIGHT OF WHAT THE DEAD TELL US

I was a devout Christian for most of my life. For me, the hardest thing to accept about the afterlife evidence was the fact that it so blatantly contradicts most of the tenets of mainstream Christianity. It was only when I reread the Gospel words of Jesus in light of what I had learned from the afterlife evidence that I realized that two thousand years ago Jesus shared with us truths about God, reality, death, the afterlife, and the meaning and purpose of human life that we could not have confirmed independently until at least the twentieth century. Thanks to modern afterlife communications, now we can prove that Jesus is real! He tells us repeatedly in the Gospels that He came to us as our teacher, and at last we can see what He meant to teach.

The afterlife evidence indicates that a lot of what mainstream Christianity teaches is based in human ideas. The dead don't sleep until they hear a final trumpet. Their bodies don't reassemble out of the soil. Being baptized does not matter after death; having taken communion does not matter; and accepting Jesus as our personal savior makes no discernible afterlife difference. Evidence suggests that practicing any religion in life does not matter after death, but what counts for us when we die is whether or not we have elevated ourselves spiritually away from fear and toward more perfect love. And wonderfully, the easiest way to do that is for us to live our lives in accordance with Jesus's Gospel teachings.

Jesus tells us to **"Ask, and it will be given to you; seek, and you will find"** (LK 9:11). So I asked. I urge you to do the same! And I see this as a matter of some urgency now, since the afterlife realities are as real as is this material universe. As good communications are developed between this material level and the higher-frequency levels where most of the dead reside, it will become clear that mainstream Christianity has not been teaching what is factual. If believers begin to turn away from Christianity, we don't want them also turning away from Jesus.

Reading Jesus's Gospel Teachings

Think how extraordinary it is that we have the two-thousand-year-old words of Someone who claimed to understand reality and to know what happens when we die. Now add the fact that most of what Jesus says in the Gospels is consistent with what we can only now deduce from afterlife communications and cutting-edge science. This gives us some amazing validations of both the teachings of Jesus and the modern evidence! Such an extensive coincidence is so unlikely as to be for practical purposes impossible. Yet if you share my wonder and delight at finding how well the words of Jesus fit the evidence, I have to remind you that the odds are long against our having available to us exactly what Jesus said.

Many Christians consider the entire Christian Bible to be the Inspired Word of God. Having read it through a number of times, I must tell you that I find the Bible to be so internally inconsistent and so full of culturally-biased and even un-Christian advice that it seems presumptuous and insulting to pin it all on God. It seems more accurate to say that the writers whose work was assembled into the Christian Bible may have been inspired by God, but they heard God through the filter of their primitive lives in the ancient world so they could have garbled some of God's message. This would be understandable and forgivable. But the fact that it might have happened means that no serious researcher can use most of the Bible as a resource when trying to understand a factual God.

The red letters of the Gospels are another matter. Thomas Jefferson said that the words of Jesus stand out in the Bible "like diamonds in a dunghill," and when you read the Bible through and reach the Gospels, you can see what he meant. In a modern translation, Jesus sounds like a man of today trying to educate primitives: you see Him speaking simply and patiently, saying things over and over to people who seem not really to understand Him. You even see his rising frustration, and His repeated efforts to quell that frustration and say things over yet again, more simply. Put aside the fact that Jesus's followers started in His name a prominent and now widely fragmented religion. Just read the words of Jesus without religious bias, and you find yourself sympathizing and liking Him as a wonderfully wise and good man you would enjoy having as your friend. Reading His words without religious bias makes you wonder whether things that He said might be found to be factually accurate.

Here is where our problems arise. If we don't want to indulge in the magic-thinking notion that the whole Bible is the Inspired Word of God, then we have to take into account how easily the teachings of Jesus could have been distorted during the past two thousand years. Consider:

1) **For Jesus to speak against the prevailing religion was a crime punishable by death.** He was trying to stay alive on earth long enough to share what He had come to teach, and He managed that feat for more than three years by using some fascinating tricks. He would tell what sounded like innocent stories, then say, "he who has ears to hear, let him hear" (wink-wink) to urge his followers to look for His

deeper messages. He would give people innocuous-sounding bits of information at various spots along the way, knowing that the nearby guards would change, and hoping that His faithful followers would be able to put those bits together. He would recite some important Old Testament passage, then add to it a sentence that could transform its meaning.

2) **Those who heard Jesus speak and passed his words along, and those who eventually committed them to writing, seem not always to have fully understood what He was saying.** It is possible that they inserted or altered words or passages here and there to better support their own understandings. We would be none the wiser.

3) **Jesus's messages could have been altered as they were translated into Greek and then from Greek into English.** Aramaic is so different from Greek that direct translations from Aramaic to English are nearly unrecognizable by people who are used to modern Bible versions. The fact that the Gospel words of Jesus that have been translated twice are so consistent with the afterlife evidence is flat-out amazing to me.

4) **We depend on the good will of those who were in control of the written Gospels for two millennia.** Here is where our trust is tested! There is evidence that people eager to support their own religious doctrines edited the Gospels over the years, which means that apparently words were put into or taken out of Jesus's mouth. This, too, makes the close correspondence between the surviving Gospel words of Jesus and modern afterlife communications a source of wonder and delight for us all.

A few of Jesus's Gospel words are lumps of coal among the diamonds. For example, He talks about a fiery hell, sheep and goats, and End Times Judgment; He dictates how His followers should resolve church issues, and He calls Peter the rock on which He will build His church. Passages like these are often anachronistic, inconsistent with afterlife-related evidence, and also inconsistent with the rest of Jesus's Gospel teachings, so they are clearly later edits. If we ignore these atypical bits, then what we have left in all four Gospels is a message that is stunningly consistent with modern afterlife evidence. The Man clearly knew what He was talking about, since His words agree with modern evidence in ways that could not have been known – and, indeed, might not have been liked – by the people who preserved them.

Let us imagine that we are only now finding the Gospel words of Jesus, and we know nothing about the religion that was later established in His name. We can see from afterlife-related evidence that two thousand years ago Jesus was familiar with facts about God, reality, death, the afterlife, and the meaning and purpose of human life that have come to light only recently. If all that we had were His newly found teachings, the afterlife evidence, and the afterlife science, how might we now interpret Jesus's words?

He Taught Us About God

Jesus told us the fundamental fact that God is loving Spirit, and each of us is part of God. This was radical stuff in ancient times, when most people worshiped semi-physical gods who were more like the Old Testament's Jehovah, often vengeful and hard to placate.

"God is spirit, and his worshipers must worship in spirit and in truth" (JN 4:24).

"The kingdom of God is within you" (LK 17:20-21).

"The Spirit gives life; the flesh counts for nothing. The words I have spoken to you are spirit, and they are life" (JN 6:63).

"If you love me, you will obey what I command. And I will ask the Father, and he will give you another Counselor to be with you forever – the Spirit of truth. The world cannot accept him, because it neither sees him nor knows him. But you know him, for he lives with you and will be in you" (JN 14:15-17).

Jesus took the ancient Hebrews' radical concept of a single nonphysical God and transformed it into what modern evidence shows us is universal Spirit (or Mind).

He Taught Us the Importance of Love

Jesus reduced the Old Testament's Ten Commandments to one commandment: that we learn how to love.

"A new command I give you: Love one another. As I have loved you, so you must love one another" (JN 13:34).

"'Love the Lord your God with all your heart and with all your soul and with all your mind.' This is the first and greatest commandment. And the second is like it: 'Love your neighbor as yourself.' All the Law and the Prophets hang on these two commandments" (MT 22:37-40).

"You have heard that it was said, 'Love your neighbor and hate your enemy.' But I tell you: love your enemies and pray for those who persecute you, that you may be sons of your Father in heaven... Be perfect, therefore, as your heavenly Father is perfect" (MT 5:43-48).

He Taught Us the Importance of Forgiveness

When I first realized that God does not judge us, I worried that on this point Jesus might have been mistaken. But then I considered this series of quotations.

"For if you forgive men when they sin against you, your heavenly Father will also forgive you. But if you do not forgive men their sins, your Father will not forgive your sins" (MT 6:14-15).

"Moreover, the Father judges no one, but has entrusted all judgment to the Son, that all may honor the Son just as they honor the Father" (JN 5:21-23).

"You judge by human standards; I pass judgment on no one" (JN 8:15).

"As for the person who hears my words but does not keep them, I do not judge him. For I did not come to judge the world, but to save it" (JN 12:47).

Were these messages inconsistencies? I think not. Instead, I think they were Jesus's efforts (meted out in bits at different times beneath the Temple's radar) to wean his primitive listeners from their old idea of God as judge so they could better comprehend what modern evidence tells us is true: each of us will be our own post-death judge. Jesus's disciple, Peter, asked him, "Lord, how many times shall I forgive my brother when he sins against me? Up to seven times?" Jesus answered, **"I tell you, not seven times, but seventy-seven times"** (MT 18:21-23). He even hinted pretty strongly that each of us will judge ourselves:

"Do not judge, or you too will be judged. For in the same way you judge others, you will be judged, and with the measure you use, it will be measured to you" (MT 7:1-2).

He Taught Us the Need for Humility

Into that ancient class-obsessed world Jesus brought a rude shock for the elite: after we die, our status in life means nothing.

"Many who are first will be last, and the last first" (MK 10:31).

"The greatest among you will be your servant. For whoever exalts himself will be humbled, and whoever humbles himself will be exalted" (MT 23:11-12).

"Whoever welcomes this little child in my name welcomes me, and whoever welcomes me welcomes the one who sent me. For he who is least among you all – he is the greatest" (LK 9:48).

"Let the little children come to me, and do not hinder them, for the kingdom of God belongs to such as these. I tell you the truth, anyone who will not receive The kingdom of God like a little child will never enter it" (MK 10:14-15).

He Taught Us About the Power of Our Minds

Mainstream Christian doctrines ignore something that strikes a modern nonreligious reader: Jesus said a lot about the power of our minds to affect reality.

"Take heart, daughter. Your faith has healed you" (MT 9:22).

(Healing a blind man) **"Do you believe that I am able to do this?... According to your faith will it be done to you"** (MT 9:28-29).

(When Peter couldn't walk on water) **"You of little faith. Why did you doubt?"** (MT 14:31)

"Who touched me? Someone touched me. I know that power has gone out from me... Daughter, your faith has healed you. Go in peace" (LK 8:46-48).

"Have faith in God. I tell you the truth, if anyone says to this mountain, 'Go, throw yourself into the sea,' and does not doubt in his heart but believes that what he says will happen, it will be done for him. Therefore I tell you, whatever you ask for in prayer, believe that you have received it, and it will be yours" (MK 11:22-24).

It is difficult for us to appreciate how radical these teachings were in the Judea and Samaria of two thousand years ago! Jesus used the familiar Hebrew concept of faith in God to teach His followers the power of their eternal minds, and to teach them that their minds – like His – were part of one universal Mind.

"When you pray, go into your room, close the door and pray to your Father, who is unseen. Then your Father, who sees what is done in secret, will reward you" (MT 6:6).

"For whatever is hidden is meant to be disclosed, and whatever is concealed is meant to be brought out into the open. If anyone has ears to hear, let him hear" (MK 4:22-23).

He Taught Us About the Afterlife

Some of the messages attributed to Jesus seem inexplicable and even cruel until we compare them with the afterlife evidence. That is when we realize that Jesus was talking not about this life, but about the afterlife. He was right in telling us that spiritual development is our real goal, and right in saying that there is no way to shortcut it. He was right, too, in saying that those who don't progress sufficiently may regress and lose whatever progress they have made, and they may even judge and condemn themselves to the dark and smelly lowest afterlife level, which he referred to as the outer darkness.

"For everyone who has will be given more, and he will have an abundance. Whoever does not have, even what he has will be taken from him. And throw that worthless servant outside, into the darkness, where there will be weeping and gnashing of teeth" (MT 29:30).

"For there is nothing hidden that will not be disclosed, and nothing concealed that will not be known or brought out into the open. Therefore consider carefully how you listen. Whoever has will be given more; whoever does not have, even what he thinks he has will be taken from him" (LK 8:17-18).

When Jesus mentions "having" in these places, He isn't talking about material things. He is referring to spiritual growth, which from His perspective is the one thing worth having.

Jesus told us about the tremendous size of the afterlife. He told us about our eternal progress. He even told us that our loved ones would create after-death homes for us, and would meet us at our deaths and take us there.

"In my father's house are many rooms; if it were not so, I would have told you. I am going there to prepare a place for you. And if I go and prepare a place for you, I will come back and take you to be with me that you also may be where I am. You know the way to the place where I am going" (JN 14:2-4).

"Blessed are the poor in spirit, for theirs is the kingdom of heaven.... Blessed are the pure in heart, for they will see God" (MT 5:3, 8).

His Teachings Are a Prescription for Spiritual Advancement

The law of spiritual advancement is implacable. Contrary to modern Christian teachings about "salvation" resulting from the death of Jesus, Jesus Himself is exactly right: there are no shortcuts. Much of what Jesus says in the Gospels can be read as lessons in better controlling your mind.

"Do not resist an evil person. If someone strikes you on the right cheek, turn to him the other also. And if someone wants to sue you and take your tunic, let him have your cloak as well. If someone forces you to go one mile, go with him two miles" (MT 5:39-41).

"You have heard that it was said to the people long ago, 'Do not murder, and anyone who murders will be subject to judgment.' But I tell you that anyone who is angry with his brother will be subject to judgment. Again, anyone who says to his brother, 'Raca,' is answerable to the Sanhedrin" (MT 5:21-22).

"Why do you look at the speck of sawdust in your brother's eye and pay no attention to the plank in your own eye? How can you say to your brother, 'Brother, let me take the speck out of your eye,' when you yourself fail to see the plank in your own eye? You hypocrite, first take the plank out of your eye, and then you will see clearly to remove the speck from your brother's eye" (LK 6:41-42).

"If any one of you is without sin, let him be the first to throw a stone at her" (JN 8:7).

"But love your enemies, do good to them, and lend to them without expecting to get anything back. Then your reward will be great, and you will be sons of the Most High, because he is kind to the ungrateful and wicked. Be merciful, just as your Father is merciful" (LK 6:35-36).

Jesus shared wonderful parables about spiritual growth. We know them as the tales of the Good Samaritan, the Keeper of the

Vineyard, and the Prodigal Son. In every way that He could, He urged his listeners to keep striving for spiritual perfection.

"I tell you that in the same way there is more rejoicing in heaven over one sinner who repents than over ninety-nine righteous persons who do not need to repent" (LK 15:7).

He Did Not Like Clergymen or Religious Traditions

Jesus was kind to everyone. He loved even lepers and tax collectors, at a time when lepers were shunned by all and tax collectors were evil incarnate. The only people who griped him were clergymen. He was bothered by not just their fake piety and self-importance, but also their religious traditions.

"Watch out for the teachers of the law. They like to walk around in flowing robes and be greeted in the marketplaces, and have the most important seats in the synagogues and the places of honor at banquets. They devour widows' houses and for a show make lengthy prayers. Such men will be punished most severely" (MK 12:38-40).

"And why do you break the command of God for the sake of your tradition? ...You hypocrites! Isaiah was right when he prophesied about you: 'These people honor me with their lips, but their hearts are far from me. They worship me in vain; their teachings are but rules taught by men'" (MT 15:3-9).

"You have let go of the commands of God and are holding on to the traditions of men... You have a fine way of setting aside the commands of God in order to observe your own traditions" (MK 7:8-9).

"Be careful not to do your 'acts of righteousness' before men, to be seen by them. If you do, you will have no reward from your

Father in heaven. So when you give to the needy, do not announce it with trumpets, as the hypocrites do in the synagogues and on the streets, to be honored by men. I tell you the truth, they have received their reward in full. But when you give to the needy, do not let your left hand know what your right hand is doing, so that your giving may be in secret. Then your father, who sees what is done in secret, will reward you. When you pray, do not be like the hypocrites, for they love to pray standing in the synagogues and on the street corners to be seen by men. I tell you the truth, they have received their reward in full. When you pray, go into your room, close the door and pray to your Father, who is unseen. Then your Father, who sees what is done in secret, will reward you" (MT 6:1-6).

Does this sound like someone who was trying to establish His own religion? Or was He instead telling us that we don't need religions at all, but we can approach God individually, since each of us is part of one universal Mind? Jesus's teachings are profoundly individual.

"Ask, and it will be given to you; seek, and you will find; knock, and the door will be opened to you. For everyone who asks receives; he who seeks finds; and to him who knocks, the door is opened" (LK 11:9-10).

"Not everyone who says to me, 'Lord, Lord,' will enter the kingdom of heaven, but only he who does the will of my Father who is in heaven" (MT 7:21).

"Why do you call me 'Lord, Lord,' and do not do what I say?" (LK 6:46)

"If you hold to my teaching, you are really my disciples. Then you will know the truth, and the truth will set you free" (JN 8:31-32).

It amazes me that so little has been made of the fact that this perfectly loving man seems to have had an aversion to religions. Does it not seem possible that, far from establishing yet one more religion, Jesus was trying to "set you free" from religions altogether?

His Death Was Not Meant to Save Us from God's Wrath

I have a confession to make. I have always found it hard to believe that a perfectly loving God would demand the blood-sacrifice of His own child. Whenever I asked clergymen about it, they would say it was "a sacred mystery." I know better now. *The afterlife evidence tells us that accepting Jesus as one's personal savior is not necessary for anyone to get into heaven. And neither God nor any religious figure ever is our afterlife judge.* So if Jesus didn't die as a blood-sacrifice to redeem us from God's punishment for our sins, then what else might have been the purpose of His dramatic death and resurrection?

Jesus Himself tells us that He was demonstrating for simple people the good news that death is not real.

Jesus's Message Is Not That Being a Christian Is the Only Way to be "Saved"

As the Roman version of Christianity developed, Christians became convinced that Jesus had said that accepting Him as one's personal savior was the only way to get into heaven.

"I am the way, the truth and the life. No one comes to the Father except through me" (JN 14:6).

"I am the resurrection and the life. He who believes in me will live, even though he dies; and whoever lives and believes in me will never die" (JN 11:25-26).

Afterlife evidence does not support this Christians-only reading of His words, but it would support another reading. Simply replace "I" and "me" with "my teachings":

"My teachings are the way, the truth and the life. No one comes to the Father except through My teachings."

"My teachings are the resurrection and the life. He who believes in My teachings will live, even though he dies; and whoever lives and believes in My teachings will never die."

Jesus so persistently emphasized our need to follow His teachings that this revised reading makes more sense anyway. Perhaps those who heard Him misunderstood Him. Or perhaps later custodians of His words altered them to better support developing Christian doctrines. Unfortunately, in reliance on those altered words, Jesus's followers soon were torturing and murdering and committing mayhem in His name, in utter contravention of His teachings! No conversion effort has been considered too brutal to be used, if making people Christian was the only way to "save" them.

But Jesus told us repeatedly that following His teachings is what matters!

"What do you think? There was a man who had two sons. He went to the first and said, 'Son, go and work today in the vineyard.' 'I will not,' he answered, but later he changed his mind and went. Then the father went to the other son and said the same thing. He answered, 'I will, sir,' but he did not go. Which of the two did what his father wanted?... I tell you the truth, the tax collectors and the prostitutes are entering the kingdom of God ahead of you" (MT 21:28-31).

"I say to you that many will come from the east and the west, and will take their places at the feast with Jacob in the kingdom of heaven. But the subjects of the kingdom will be thrown outside, into the darkness, where there will be weeping and gnashing of teeth" (MT 8:11-12).

Most comforting of all His words are these:

"I shall be with you always, to the very end of the age" (MT 28:20).

What Was His Mission?

Jesus was speaking to primitive people steeped in superstitious terrors, and ignorant of nearly everything that you and I consider to be commonplace. His teachings for them were simple, even simplistic. We severely underestimate the Man if we suppose that if He walked the earth today, He would express himself to us as He expressed himself to them! If we keep this fact in mind, then in light of modern afterlife evidence we can develop a pretty good sense of what Jesus came to earth to do.

I think Jesus's life had a four-fold purpose.

First, He came to tell us what God is.

Second, He came to show us that life is eternal.

Third, He came to give us a taste of what the afterlife is like.

Finally, He came to teach us how to make the most spiritual progress while we are on Earth.

If these were His objectives, then His death and resurrection can be seen as a loving and joyous "Ta-da!"

At last, two thousand years ago, human beings were ready to start to learn what modern afterlife evidence has only now revealed to us, two very bloody millennia later. Had His followers fully understood what He was saying at the time, human history could have been so different!

Mainstream Christianity does not own Jesus, just as no religion owns God. Surely He deserves another chance to be heard in light of modern afterlife evidence. Paul and the other New Testament writers did a good job of wrapping Jesus's teachings in Hebrew prophesy so they could be preserved for two thousand years. **Thank you, Paul! Now at last we can open your gift.**

APPENDIX V
SIXTEEN CHRISTIAN BELIEFS THAT HAVE A HUMAN ORIGIN

In light of what our dead communicators have told us, and in light of the Gospel testimony of Jesus Himself, let's look now at sixteen Christian teachings and beliefs that are frankly erroneous:

- **God is a human-like individual with a beard.** Those that we used to think were dead consistently tell us that God is perfectly loving energy. Jesus Himself said, **"God is Spirit, and those who worship Him must worship in spirit and truth"** (JN 4:24). God has no human failings, and God never takes a body. My preferred definition after a lifetime of study is that God is "an infinitely powerful energy-like potentiality without size or form, alive in the sense that your mind is alive, highly emotional and therefore probably self-aware." Mikey Morgan, who is the highest-level recently-dead being of whom I am aware, insists simply that God is "the unity of pure love and all that exists." Quantum physicist Max Planck said that what we experience as human consciousness – he called it "mind" – is the source of everything. But no matter how we might end up defining the Source, it is clear that God is not just a bigger and more powerful version of fallible us!

- **Sin is wrongdoing.** Those that we used to think were dead tell us that sin is a human word. It is the breaking of human rules, when in fact with God there are no rules beyond the law of perfect love. After our deaths we will be judged by ourselves based exclusively on whether each thing that we have done in our lives was loving or unloving.

- **God judges us.** The insistence among Christians on believing that God judges us is especially ridiculous, when Jesus tells us flat-out in the Gospels that it simply is not true! Of course, He had to hedge the way He said it because those Temple guards were always listening. To preach against Jewish beliefs was a capital crime, so one of the things that He often did was to give His followers truths over days of time. One day He said, **"For not even the Father judges anyone, but He has given all judgment to the Son, so that all will honor the Son even as they honor the Father"** (JN 5:22-23). Then after He got that little revelation past the guards, on a different day and with different guards present He said, **"If anyone hears My sayings and does not keep them, I do not judge him; for I did not come to judge the world, but to save the world"** (JN 12:47). Of course, since He has already told us that God never judges us, Jesus could not have come to save us from God's judgment. What He came to save us from was the desperate spiritual ignorance that is the greatest threat that humankind even now faces.

- **Jesus died for our sins.** When there is in fact no such thing as divinely-described sin, and when anyway God never judges us, the core Christian doctrine of substitutionary atonement is out the window. In all my years of looking for it, I never have found a single instance where the death of Jesus on the cross has ever made an afterlife difference for a single human being.

- **Roman Christianity helps you to grow spiritually.** Reality is entirely consciousness-based. Consciousness exists in a range of vibrations from the lowest, which is fear, to the highest, which is perfect love. Since Christianity, like all religions, is based in fear of God and the devil, fear of hell, and fear of adverse outcomes if we don't toe the religious line, Christianity as it is now practiced makes your spiritual growth a lot more difficult. Fortunately, the genuine teachings of Jesus which are contained (but ignored) in the Christian Bible are the easiest and most effective plan for achieving rapid spiritual growth that ever has been given to us, so if you simply ignore all the false Christian dogmas and instead closely follow the teachings of Jesus you are doing the best that you can for this lifetime.

- **God might condemn us to spend eternity in a fiery hell.** In all my years of looking for it, I have found no evidence whatsoever for either a fiery hell or permanent damnation. The lowest vibratory level of the afterlife is what Jesus called the "outer darkness," cold and dark and smelly and populated by demon-like people who have let their spiritual vibratory rate sink so low that now they cannot go above that level. It is a punishment level of sorts, but researchers have found no evidence that we are put there by anyone but ourselves.

- **The Old Testament rules still apply.** No they don't. Not only are they sin-based and therefore of human and not divine origin, but Jesus in the Gospels specifically threw out the entire Old Testament and replaced it with God's law of love. He said, **"'You shall love the Lord your God with all your heart, and with all your soul, and with all your mind.' This is the great and foremost commandment. The second is like it, 'You shall love your neighbor as yourself.' On these two commandments depend the whole Law and the Prophets"** (MT 22:37-40). "The Law and the Prophets" was what the Jews of His day called all the Old Testament books. Jesus also specifically told His followers not to package His teachings in their old religion! He said, **"But no one puts a patch of unshrunk cloth on an old garment; for the patch pulls away from the garment, and a worse tear results. Nor do people put new wine into old wineskins; otherwise the wineskins burst, and the wine pours out and the wineskins are ruined; but they put new wine into fresh wineskins, and both are preserved"** (MT 9:16-17). If you have a pair of scissors handy, you can vastly improve your Bible by cutting away the entire wineskin of the Old and most of the New Testaments, and then from now on you can read just the true Gospels wine.
- **Only Christians get into heaven.** According to nearly two hundred years of abundant and consistent afterlife evidence, everybody gets into heaven. In fact, the evidence indicates that some of those who have the

most trouble with their afterlife transitions are closed-minded Christians who might put themselves into what are called "hollow heavens," darkish places in the astral plane that are outside the general afterlife process, where nothing exists but their own religious practice. Being in a hollow heaven is vastly boring, but fortunately sooner or later all these off-track people will be rescued.

- **God is a Trinity.** The Trinity idea is a human construct that was popular in several ancient cultures around the time that Roman Christianity was first created, and it was imported into Christianity as a kind of marketing feature, just as a lot of human nonsense was imported into Christianity. For example, the Egyptian equivalent of the Father, Son and Holy Ghost are said to have been Osiris, Isis, and Horus. In reality, there is one Source energy, and all our minds are part of that Source energy, so not only is God not a trinity, but in reality God and all human beings who ever have lived are indivisibly parts of one Whole! The notion of the Trinity is harmful to our spiritual growth because it is all about separate divine entities trying to come together in various ways, when in reality there are no separations at all.

- **Some people are "Elect" and some are not.** Simply put, this is human-made, bogus, and highly negative nonsense.

- **The Christian Bible is the Inspired Word of God.** What eventually became your Christian Bible was first assembled by the Council of Nicaea in 325, using books chosen from an array of possibilities. They claimed that what they were assembling was the Inspired Word of God, but in fact it is the result of a lot of politicking and back-room dealing. In the same way that if you like hot dogs you are warned not to watch them being made, so if you want to love the Bible you must never study the Council of Nicaea! The result of the Council's work is so full of frank inconsistencies and outright barbarity that it is impossible for it to have been the work of the genuine, perfectly loving and eternal God.

- **Satan is a powerful evil entity.** Those that we used to think were dead consistently tell us that no powerful evil entity exists in opposition to God. There are low-vibration nasties not in bodies who can give us trouble if we allow ourselves to be weakened spiritually; but unless we encourage them, they cannot do much to harm us. And this is of course entirely consistent with what we know about consciousness. The higher its vibratory rate – the closer it is to perfect love – the more powerful it is; but the lower it vibrates – the closer it is to abject fear and negativity – the weaker it is. We believe that the most evil entities of all are the shadow men, dark wraiths who often wear top hats and long capes, and they are so weak that they disappear in anything but very dim light. Their only way to maintain enough power to even very barely exist is to feed on more negativity, so they often lurk in closets of susceptible people and pop out to scare them. Some pathetic evil that is! Just keeping a nightlight on will banish them altogether.

- **Jesus will return in an end-times war.** The centuries following the death of Jesus were a time of Christian persecution that gave rise to the belief that Jesus was about to come back and save His followers; and that belief in turn gave rise to a genre of end-times revenge literature. As the Council of Nicaea assembled what became the Christian Bible in 325, they chose to include one of the worst of these screeds as the Biblical Book of Revelation. The whole thing defies common sense! Are we to believe that the eternal Son of God entered a voluntary lifetime so He could teach us how to raise our spiritual vibrations and bring the Kingdom of God on earth; and then less than a century after His death, He said, "Oops! Never mind," and promised to come right back and fight an end-times war? The whole idea makes Jesus look ridiculous! He would know that such a war would drastically *lower* the spiritual vibration of the planet, thereby negating whatever good effect His teachings might have had. So you won't be surprised to learn that those that we used to think were dead insist that the whole end-times war thing is a manmade construct. They tell us that it never is going to happen, but just a little knowledge of the Gospels and the afterlife evidence combined with simple common sense would assure us of that fact in any event.

- **"Saved" People Will be Raptured Before Armageddon.** Of course, without an end-times war there won't be a Rapture either, but the origin of this predicted event is entirely human, anyway. The term "Rapture" does not appear in the Bible, and even the few touted Biblical references to what is assumed to be a rapture-like event seem to be that only in retrospect. The popularization of the idea of a Rapture of the "saved" in order to protect them from the end-times tribulations seems to have begun in the 1830s, and reportedly it had its origins in a dream that a teenage girl shared with her pastor.

- **Jesus founded Christianity.** There is no doubt that Jesus came to start a movement, but nothing about His Gospel words suggests that what He meant to start would even resemble the Christianity that was begun three centuries after His death. He explicitly told us not to package His teachings with other ideas and beliefs, which is precisely what Paul and the early church councils did! Jesus said, **"But no one puts a patch of unshrunk cloth on an old garment; for the patch pulls away from the garment, and a worse tear results. Nor do people put new wine into old wineskins; otherwise the wineskins burst, and the wine pours out and the wineskins are ruined; but they put new wine into fresh wineskins, and both are preserved"** (MT 9:16-17). He even urged Jewish clergymen who had adopted His teachings as true to keep them separate from the religion being practiced. He said, **"Therefore every scribe who has become a disciple of the kingdom of heaven is like a head of a household, who brings out of his treasure things new and old"** (MT 13:52).

- **God is going to be giving us no further information about anything.** Devout Christians are appallingly closed-minded about the possibility that God might ever want to give us new revelation. Over the past two thousand years we have seen major advancements in every area of human life and culture, but still we require that God remain stuck two millennia into the past? Who are we to deny God the right to continue to reveal greater truths to His people as our understanding progresses?

What Christian beliefs are left standing now? Not many. Nothing except the genuine teachings of Jesus as they are preserved in the Gospels. Fortunately, though, those teachings are enough.

APPENDIX VI
A BRIEF OVERVIEW OF THE AFTERLIFE EVIDENCE

W e have nearly two hundred years of astonishingly varied afterlife evidence. And just as important as the volume and variety of this evidence is the fact that it is so consistent, and when we put it together we begin to glimpse a wonderfully complex and beautiful reality that dwarfs this material universe. Indeed, the greater reality just now coming into view might be as much as twenty times the size of our universe! It is all beyond amazing, and far beyond thrilling.

I recommend that you read Victor and Wendy Zammit's important book, *A Lawyer Presents the Evidence for the Afterlife*, and that you also peruse some of the seventy-odd books listed in the Appendix II annotated bibliography. To help you get started, I will here list in no particular order some of the kinds of evidence that I have used in assembling my understanding of death, the afterlife, and the greater reality in which we live:

- *Communications Received Through Deep-Trance Mediums.* These mediums are able to withdraw from their bodies sufficiently to let the dead use their vocal cords to speak. And the testimony of the best evidence received this way is such that if mainstream physicists had not a century ago already been dogmatically materialist, the fact that you will survive your death would long ago have become common knowledge.

- *Communications Received Through Physical Mediums.* There are mediums who have developed their skills to such an extent that they can go into deep trance and facilitate the production of voices, sounds, and even our loved ones present in the room.

- *Communications Received Through Mental Mediums.* This is an area where double- and triple-blind scientific studies are possible, and these studies demonstrate that some mental mediums indeed are in contact with the dead. The work of the best mental mediums has produced a wealth of interesting and consistent information.

- *Accounts Received Through Automatic Writing.* Sometimes a medium can invite a dead person to write using the medium's hands. I have read a few accounts that were written this way, and have found them to be so consistent with the information that I have assembled from other sources that I consider the few that I have read to be likely genuine.

- *Channeled Accounts.* Throughout history, there have been mediums who have received in one way or another entire books that they claimed came from dead people, and that purportedly gave us the straight skinny on what is really going on. I have mistrusted most channeled work, so it is a humbling irony that I have lately been made to understand that all my own books have been channeled. Never say that God lacks a sense of humor!

- *Consciousness Research.* To this day, mainstream scientists are so stuck in their "fundamental scientific dogma of materialism" that they are obsessed with trying to find a source of consciousness inside the human brain. Since consciousness is the source of reality, this is the equivalent of studying a radio to try to figure out how it makes the voice of Frank Sinatra, but fortunately there are some adventurous physicists who have done groundbreaking research that pretty well indicates what consciousness is and how it operates as the basic source of all reality.

- *Deathbed Visions.* Those who are dying will often have extraordinary experiences that include visits from dead loved ones and occasional glimpses of the places where they will be going after death.

- *Accounts by Out-of-Body Travelers.* There is a lot of evidence that we travel out of our bodies often during sleep, but to learn to do it while we are awake is difficult. There are some, though, who have demonstrated an ability to travel out of their bodies at will, and the published accounts by out-of-body travelers who have explored the greater astral reality are remarkably consistent with the rest of the evidence.

- *General Scientific Research.* From enigmas like dark matter and energy and the Big Bang, through to the troubling fact that "solid" matter is not solid, modern scientific inquiry remains severely hamstrung by its obsession with materialism as a dogma. At the same time, scientific researchers continue to turn out consistent bits of information that help afterlife researchers as we build our increasingly detailed picture of the greater reality.

- *Ghosts and Disembodied Spirits.* These are areas so repugnant to me that I try not even to think about them, but little by little I have felt forced to investigate the phenomena of hauntings and also influence or possession by low-vibration entities. And, yes, what we are learning there fits the overall factual picture that we are building.

- *Hypnotic Regression and Progression.* Some therapists help their patients regress or progress to what appear to be past or future lives, and thereby help them to resolve some psychological ailments. In doing so, they have uncovered some fascinating, and consistent, information.

- *Instrumental Transcommunication (ITC) Including Electronic Voice Phenomena (EVP).* Communicating with the dead by means of computers, tape recorders, telephones, televisions, and various "black box" devices is a very promising area that has yet to bear much fruit, in part because few living researchers are able to devote the necessary time to conducting experiments at the direction of dead researchers. And occasionally, squabbling among living researchers will cause their dead collaborators to withdraw. More recently, we have come to understand that there also are some very bad nonmaterial entities who are trying to keep reliable communication between the living and the dead from ever happening. Knowing what is wrong is half of solving the problem. Expect reliable electronic communication with the dead to be in place before 2050.

- *Near-Death Experiences.* We are told by those that we used to think were dead that people who have near-death experiences don't go to the places where the dead reside, but they generally travel out of their bodies and they often have remarkable experiences. When we understand and stipulate that the events depicted in near-death experiences are not indicative of afterlife facts, we can study just the mechanics of NDEs. And there we find information that is entirely consistent with what we have learned from other sources.

- *Past-Life Memories of Children.* Some toddlers appear to have memories of recent past lives that ended violently. These cases seem to me to be less evidence for general reincarnation than they are suggestions of what might perhaps go wrong in the process of transition.

- *Quantum Physics.* The physics of the places where the dead reside is so different from the physics of this level of reality that until good quantum-physics-for-dummies books became available early in this century, afterlife researchers had trouble making sense of it all. It turns out that quantum physics is apparently a kind of plug that connects what we might think of as the mathematics-based physics of this level of reality with the consciousness-based physics that exists in perhaps ninety-five percent of the greater reality that even physicists are aware must exist. Thanks to those who have made the principles of quantum mechanics understandable to people who never got beyond Algebra II, afterlife researchers are coming to understand a lot more about how reality is put together and how it seems to work.

- *Work of Independent Scientists.* Nearly all researchers in the field of afterlife studies are lawyers, psychologists, and other laypeople. We revere those few trained scientists who during the past century have come across data that suggested there was a lot more going on than what was currently being studied. Despite the strong stigma in scientific circles that still exists against scientists who don't respect the "fundamental dogma of materialism," and despite the lack of funding for researchers who venture off the materialist reservation, these visionaries have done extraordinary work in fields related to afterlife studies. And all such research results of which I am aware are consistent with what has been developed by earnest laypeople.

APPENDIX VII
A BRIEF OVERVIEW OF THE GREATER REALITY

W hat afterlife researchers have discovered is a lot more than just the happy fact that every human mind is eternal! Because the afterlife is real, our study of it has led us to the amazing discovery of a greater reality that seems to be many times the size of this material universe, and to a new kind of physics that is consciousness-based. To give you even a rudimentary understanding of the whole picture would take a separate book. So here I will just share with you brief descriptions of some of the aspects of the afterlife on which researchers generally agree.

God

No human-like God exists. Instead, the only thing that exists is an energy-like potentiality without size or form, infinitely powerful, alive in the sense that your mind is alive, highly emotional and therefore probably self-aware. And the only emotion this genuine God expresses is love beyond our ability to comprehend it. Each human mind is part of God. It is likely not wrong to say that God and all our minds together are of an energy that we experience in a limited way as human consciousness, but no one knows much about the Most High God beyond the definition given above. Everything that we think of as real is an aspect or an artifact of God. And creation, if you want to call it that, is apparently not a one-time thing. Evidence suggests that time does not exist in most of reality, and the Godhead Collective of this universe is at the top of the range of astral realties and is continuously manifesting all that we believe exists around us.

The Structure of the Greater Reality

The simplest way to envision reality is as a spectrum of energy signals very much like the television signals that are in the room around you, and to imagine your mind as a television set now tuned to that particular body on this material level of reality. We think this material reality is the lowest vibratory level, but no one is sure about that. We do know that existing at slightly higher vibratory rates are at least seven major levels and perhaps infinite minor levels of nonmaterial reality that make up what we think of as the astral plane, a part of which is what we think of as the afterlife. Each of these separate vibrational frequencies may be as big as this whole material universe, to the extent that size matters when there is no objective time or space; and all of them, like the TV signals in the room around you, are perceptible together in one place.

Nothing is solid. Everything is energy. The only thing that objectively exists is God, and every human mind is an infinitely loved part of God.

The Afterlife Levels

The afterlife is a part of the astral, and it includes at least seven primary and infinite lesser energy-based post-death levels of reality. Six of those primary levels feel as solid to their inhabitants as this material level feels to us, and all of them are in the same place, just as you can tune your TV from a lower channel to a higher channel and find there a different TV program. We can be comfortable on the highest afterlife level to which our personal degree of spiritual development suits us, but we find it unbearable to go higher. And we want to go higher! There is more to do, there are ever more pleasures on the higher vibratory levels. So the more spiritual progress you can make in this lifetime, the more kinds of fun will be available to you once you return to the greater reality that is your eternal home.

Right above the vibratory rate of matter is the lowest afterlife level, which Jesus called the outer darkness. It is the punishment level, cold and dark, smelly and repellent and populated by tormented, demon-like people; and the evidence indicates that everyone who is there essentially has put himself there. We have found no evidence of any post-death judgment by anyone but ourselves.

Just above the lowest primary afterlife level is a recovery level, still twilight-dark, but with homes and without the awful cold and stench and hopelessness of the lowest level.

Levels Three through Five of the afterlife are the beautiful Summerland levels. All three are intensely earthlike, full of enormous flowers in extraordinary colors and magnificent buildings and scenery. The higher the vibratory rate of each of these levels, the more gorgeous everything appears to be.

Primary Level Six is just below the Source. Historically the dead have called it the causal or mental level, since it is the home of spiritually advanced people who mind-create what exists in the lower afterlife levels. (I recall long ago reading an account from a sixth-level being who was frustrated by the process of learning how to create living plants. It was hilarious.) Mikey Morgan, our great friend who died in 2007 and now lives in the sixth level, refers to it as the teaching level, since for many who live at that level, spiritual teaching in the lower afterlife levels and on earth is a primary occupation. He tells us that Level Six is full of beautiful universities where very advanced beings help one another to make ever more spiritual progress.

The highest vibratory level of which we are aware is the Celestial or Source Level, which apparently is something like the center of the Godhead Collective that continuously manifests this material reality. The Celestial Level is also the source of the magnificent white light that fills most of the greater reality and makes it feel to those who are there as if they are living bathed in love.

The Death Process

Our bodies resist dying. Getting them to the point where they can no longer support life and we are released from these earthly shells can be a rough experience, as I have been reminded by some who objected to the title of my book, *The Fun of Dying*. But shortly before we leave our bodies, the fun begins as we start to see some of the people we had loved in life and thought were dead appear around our deathbed. We leave our bodies as what might appear to bedside observers to be an energy mist, and we re-form into a human shape while we are still attached to our material body by a spiritual umbilicus called the silver cord. This process of liberation is quite pleasurable, as is our joyous reunion with loved ones at our bedside. We might hardly notice the fraying of our silver cord, but as it is severed, our physical body dies. Then we are off with those we love, raising our spiritual vibratory rate to the point where a whole new solid and beautiful reality appears around us. If you will trust in the process, you will find that dying is just that easy, and just that wonderful.

Our Post-Death Life

A whole book by itself could be written about all that the dead have been pleased to tell us about their wonderful post-death lives. Here are a few highlights:

Our post-death bodies are mind-created, and most of us choose to look and feel as we did while on earth at maybe age thirty. The standard "spirit robe" is a long-sleeved, floor-length belted tunic in vibrant pastel hues, like an angel's dress; but many people prefer to wear earth-clothing. Nobody cares how you dress. Mikey Morgan, who died in 2007 at the age of 20, tells us that he wears college-kid clothes most of the time, but when he returns to the sixth level he wears his spirit robe.

Dead children and miscarried or aborted fetuses are treated like royalty, reared in beautiful homes and villages that are off-limits to any but their carefully-selected caretakers. They grow to young adulthood at their own pace, generally over just a few earth-years, and they closely follow their parents' lives and greet their eventual arrival with joy. I recall reading one early-twentieth-century communication in which a woman who apparently had had four coat-hanger abortions reported that she had been staggered to be greeted at her death by four beautiful young adults who loved her and called her their mother.

There are infinite things to do. And since night never falls and we don't need to sleep, we have close to infinite time in which to happily entertain ourselves. We travel in space and travel in time, play sports, learn to paint pictures and play the piano, research our past lives, attend Elvis concerts, take classes, boat and fly around, show up at impromptu welcoming parties, and even sit at the feet of Jesus. Mikey Morgan enjoys perfecting his snowboarding. The more spiritually advanced you are, the more options are available to you, which is another reason to take your earthly spiritual growth seriously.

All the companion animals we have loved in life are there to greet us, now young and healthy. Animals have species-specific "group souls" to which they return at death, but being loved by a human being enables them to establish an independent existence. They live in the afterlife in happy packs, or they live with your family members until you arrive. Like us, they neither eat nor eliminate, so the only care that they need now is love.

And yes, I do understand that all of this seems too good to be true. You are coming home hoping for milk and cookies and comfort after your rough day at school, and what you get instead is a three-ring circus of ponies and elephants and aerial acts and every earthly pleasure. As I have read so many wonderful accounts, sometimes I could envision the heavenly host sort of chortling together with glee as they thought up ever more treats that you in particular might enjoy. It is impossible for you to grasp the infinite extent to which you are perfectly loved!

ISBN 9781737410669

51695 >

9 781737 410669

CPSIA information can be obtained
at www.ICGtesting.com
Printed in the USA
BVHW062155200223
658846BV00022B/698